T0301752

Accelerating Digital Transformation of SMEs

Accelerating Digital Transformation of SMEs

Clarence Goh
Yuanto Kusnadi
Benjamin Lee
Gary Pan
Poh Sun Seow

Singapore Management University, Singapore

World Scientific

NEW JERSEY · LONDON · SINGAPORE · BEIJING · SHANGHAI · HONG KONG · TAIPEI · CHENNAI · TOKYO

Published by

World Scientific Publishing Co. Pte. Ltd.

5 Toh Tuck Link, Singapore 596224

USA office: 27 Warren Street, Suite 401-402, Hackensack, NJ 07601

UK office: 57 Shelton Street, Covent Garden, London WC2H 9HE

British Library Cataloguing-in-Publication Data
A catalogue record for this book is available from the British Library.

ISBN 978-981-127-271-4 (hardcover)
ISBN 978-981-127-272-1 (ebook for institutions)
ISBN 978-981-127-273-8 (ebook for individuals)

For any available supplementary material, please visit
https://www.worldscientific.com/worldscibooks/10.1142/13318#t=suppl

Desk Editor: Nicole Ong

Typeset by Stallion Press
Email: enquiries@stallionpress.com

Printed in Singapore

Foreword

Among businesses operating in today's environment, buzzwords such as "Digitalisation", "Artificial Intelligence", "Big Data", "Disruption" and "Transformation" are constantly in the discussions, presentations and strategic plans of business leaders. While many larger corporations like financial institutions and tech giants have embarked on their digital transformation journey since the dot com boom in the 1990s, many Asian small and medium-sized enterprises (SMEs) have only started taking small steps in the recent years and many others have yet to even start their journey.

The push for smaller business to transform digitally and adopt digital solutions now is further augmented by trends including increasing competition, availability of more advanced technologies and availability of data (coupled with lower data storage costs). Another critical factor favouring technology adoption is the increasing penetration of mobile devices which puts a "mini-computer" in everyone's palm which in turn facilitates the capturing of consumer data. The increasing prevalence of digital solutions to the masses has also altered consumer behaviour where the customer demands for quicker, more convenient and more comfortable delivery of services. This demand from the customer also pressures businesses to adopt digital solutions more quickly because if the customer demands for it and is less satisfied with traditional delivery methods, a digitally-stagnant business could risk losing the customer to a competitor who has moved forward digitally sooner.

More than 90% of global businesses are SMEs, however these businesses often lag their larger multi-national counterparts because they face a host of challenges in digital transformation. The cost of investment in technology and digital tools are often cited as a barrier to digital adoption coupled with the lack of knowledge and understanding of technology and how technology can improve the way SMEs conduct their business. Fortunately, the availability of grants and business advisors can help in advancing the digital journey of SMEs. For instance, government agencies like Enterprise Singapore support Singaporean SMEs with grants to offset initial investment into solutions under its Productivity Solutions Grants and Enterprise Development Grant programmes. Another reason why SMEs do not see their efforts in digital adoption pay off is the absence of firm commitment to change by senior leadership and users in the organisation. We know that change is immensely difficult especially when we want to change the familiar way employees are used to carrying out their daily tasks. It is hence critical that the tone from the senior leadership of an organisation help the ground users see the strategic perspective of the need to adopt new and different ways of working and how this is an inevitable move that is required for the organisation to continue to grow sustainably. Quite simply, senior leaders need to commit to the change and help their teams to believe that the change is for the better.

Most of us have been impacted by the outbreak of COVID-19 in early 2020. Despite the negative effects that the virus had on businesses and individuals, a silver lining in during the pandemic was how it compelled SMEs to accelerate their adoption of digital tools. The Chinese word for crisis (危机, *weiji*) is composed of two characters meaning "danger" and "opportunity". It was during the COVID-19 crisis that many SMEs saw the opportunity to learn new ways of doing business, improving current business processes and disrupting their respective industries. And had they not learn these new ways, some SMEs might have faced the risk of a pre-mature end to their business.

I have had the opportunity to serve as the Group Chief Operating Officer of a regional healthcare group and four months into my role, I faced the challenge of managing the impact that the COVID-19 pandemic had on our business, focussing on protecting jobs and ensuring business continuity. While many businesses came to a standstill during the various stages of COVID-19 "lock-downs", we took the downtime from the fall in business activity to plan how we can operate more efficiently and improve patient experience at our clinics. This effort to strategise and plan paid off when patient loads returned when safety measures were gradually eased.

Today we continue to look at new ways of developing digital tools including software and mobile apps as we continue with the momentum of digital transformation.

In addition to my role in the healthcare sector, I had the privilege of working with the authors of this book as an adjunct faculty member for classes that they taught at the Singapore Management University. As we mentored student projects which focussed on research and developing recommendations for real-world problems faced by SMEs in industry, in nearly every presentation done by our student teams, the recommendations will involve some form of digital solution ranging from adopting data analytics to investing in search engine optimisation/management. This shows the increasing understanding digital transformation among our youth and hopefully shape the way that they will eventually lead businesses in the future.

This book discusses how SMEs across the ASEAN have innovated business processes and leveraged on technology to disrupt industry or deal with disruption brought about by others. The short case studies provide insight to the factors that catalyse transformation undertaken by businesses across multiple industries including education, e-commerce, financial services and others. As I read this book, the commentary and insight by the authors are useful in helping me to frame discussions with stakeholders of the business that I lead. This book comes at no better time as many businesses are taking steps to transform digitally to grow as the world emerges with hope from the COVID-19 years. I hope you find the stories of businesses discussed in the book inspiring to bring about positive change to your organisation. Don't just read the book but challenge yourself to catalysing digital change.

Kevin Lee
Group Chief Operating Officer
T32 Dental Group

About the Authors

Clarence Goh is an Assistant Professor of Accounting (Practice) and Director, Professional Development at the School of Accountancy, Singapore Management University (SMU). Dr. Goh is also a Fellow of CPA Australia and a Chartered Accountant of Singapore. His research interests are in the area of judgment and decision-making in financial disclosure, financial information comparability, and data and analytics in accounting. His work has been published in international accounting journals and in media outlets, such as *CEO Magazine* and *the Business Times*.

Yuanto Kusnadi is an Associate Professor (Education) at the School of Accountancy of the Singapore Management University. He is also the Academic Director of SMU-X, under the Office of Provost. Dr. Kusnadi has won a number of international and local teaching and research awards. His research interests are on issues in corporate governance for international firms, as well as experiential and innovative teaching pedagogy. He has published articles in prestigious international journals, such as *Journal of Business, Journal of Corporate Finance, Journal of Business Ethics, Journal of Business Research, Pacific-Basin Finance Journal, Journal of Contemporary Accounting and Economics, Finance Research Letters, Journal of Financial Research, Review of Pacific-Basin Financial Markets and Policies*, and *Journal of Asia Business Studies*. His research has also been profiled in the *Asian Management Insights, Perspective@SMU, Straits Times, the Business Times, Lianhe Zaobao, SGSME, Asian Scientist*, and the *CFA Digest*. In 2021, he was the recipient of the SMU Undergraduate Teaching Excellence Award for the category of "Excellent SMU-X Teacher" and the SMU Office of Core Curriculum Annual Teaching Excellence Award: "Managing Pillar". He was also awarded the SMU Educational Research Fellow from August 2021 to December 2023.

Benjamin Lee is a Lecturer of Accounting, Director of Student Matters, and SMU-X Academic Champion of the School of Accountancy at the Singapore Management University. Benjamin is also a Chartered Accountant (Singapore). His teaching and research interests are in AI and ML for Big Data Analytics adoption, specifically in solving accounting problems including cashflow management, cost allocation, credit risk analysis, financial forecasting, fraud prediction, and inventory control. As a regular contributor to *the Business Times*, *Lianhe Zaobao*, and *ISCA Journal*, he writes on the need for accountants to embrace ML in a fast-changing world and how accountants can value-add to businesses as they adopt advanced analytics to support business functions. He is also a co-editor of a collaborative book project with CPA Australia titled "Charting the Future of Accountancy with AI" (2019) which was launched at the 8th CFO Connect Symposium and featured in *the Business Times*.

Gary Pan is a Professor of Accounting (Education) and the Associate Dean for Undergraduate and Student Development of the School of Accountancy at the Singapore Management University SOA at SMU, and also the Academic Director of Lifelong Learning. Professor Pan has published widely in peer-reviewed academic journals and professional publications. He has won a number of international and local teaching and research awards, and serves in several university and industry committees. He is a Fellow Chartered Accountant of Singapore, a Fellow of CPA Australia, and a Certified Management Accountant of Australia. He is also the Associate Editor for the *Journal of Information & Management* and an Editorial Board Member of the *Journal of Finance and Accounting*. He is also the Editor/Co-editor of five books: *Accounting & Productivity: Answering the Big Questions, Dynamics of Governing IT innovation in Singapore: A Case Book, Analytics and Cybersecurity: The Shape of Things to Come, Riding the Waves of Disruption*, and *Charting the Future of Accountancy with AI*. He is a member of the Education Committee of CPA Australia and a member of Business Management Advisory Committee, Nanyang Polytechnic School of Business Management.

Seow Poh Sun is an Associate Professor of Accounting (Education) and an Associate Dean (Teaching and Curriculum) of the School of Accountancy at the Singapore Management University. His teaching and research interests are in accounting information systems, behavioural issues in accounting and accounting education. He is a Fellow Chartered Accountant of Singapore and a Fellow of CPA Australia. Dr. Seow has won a number of international and local teaching and research awards. He was the first professor in Asia to receive the Howard Teall Award for Innovation in Accounting Education (First Prize) in 2020 from the Canadian Academic Accounting Association for his video-learning project to teach internal controls. He also received the American Accounting Association (AAA) Outstanding Instructional Contribution Award in 2018 for developing an online tutorial to teach database modelling. He also received the AAA Jim Bulloch Award for Innovations in Management Accounting Education in 2017 and the AAA Innovation in Accounting Education Award in 2015, for his award-winning mobile learning app Accounting Challenge (ACE). He and his collaborators were the first professors in Asia to win three awards from AAA. Dr. Seow was inducted into the SMU Teaching Honour Roll in 2017 for receiving at least three SMU Undergraduate Teaching Excellence Awards. He also received the SMU Teaching Excellence in Postgraduate Professional Programmes Award in 2020.

About the Contributors

Venky Shankararaman is the Vice-Provost (Education) and Professor of Information Systems (Education) at Singapore Management University. Professor Shankararaman has over 30 years of experience in the IT industry in various capacities as a researcher, academic faculty member, IT professional and industry consultant. He has published over 75 papers in academic journals and conferences. His current areas of specialization include digital business technologies and transformation, enterprise systems and integration, and education pedagogy.

Patrick Tan is a Senior Lecturer of Strategic Management and concurrently the Academic Director of International Trading Institute at Singapore Management University. Prior to joining academia, Dr. Tan has more than 30 years of management experience in the banking and insurance industry across the Asia-Pacific region. Over the years, he has taught Strategy, Business Model Innovation, Corporate Entrepreneurship, and Innovation. He earned his Ph.D from the Singapore Management University.

Contents

Prologue

Digital disruption is generally defined as the change that occurs when rapid change in digital technology and business models affects the value propositions of existing goods and services. While some recent development, such as the evolution of artificial intelligence (AI) and more prevalent usage of connected devices (i.e., Internet of Things), is clearly unsettling and present some challenges, it also offers opportunities that organisations can capitalise on.

One thing organisations can do to circumvent the digital disruption is to undergo digital transformation, which involves the integration of digital technology into business operation to create or modify existing processes. The potential benefits that can be reaped include significant cost reduction, improved financial performance and profitability, as well as better customer satisfaction.

Of course, companies need to have a framework for digital transformation which encompasses having a strong digital business strategy and culture that encourages innovation as well as effective engagement with key stakeholders (such as staff and customers). The top management needs to set strategic goals and develop roadmaps (in terms of expected outcomes) for lower-level employees to work towards the intended goals. Moreover, employees within the organisations will be required to improve their skill sets to respond to the evolving technological environment. Organisations will also need to be constantly involved in recognising the changing needs of customers and fulfilling those needs.

The ongoing COVID-19 pandemic has hastened the need for organisations to embark on digital transformation initiatives, otherwise they risk being displaced by aggressive new entrants into the market.

In this book, we have compiled several "op-eds", articles, and case studies on digital transformation initiatives involving small and medium-sized enterprises (SMEs) in Singapore, published in *the Business Times*, *Asian Management Insights*, *Perspectives@SMU*, *CPA Australia Report*, and academic journal articles in recent years.

The topics we covered in the book provide deeper insights into recent trends in digital transformations and factors influencing the implementation success of digital transformation initiatives. In addition, we also provided several case studies on how SMEs go about their digital transformation journey and the lessons that we could learn from them. We hope that these will serve as a useful resource and a starting point to encourage continuous discussion on the challenges and opportunities that digital transformation can bring to SMEs.

This book is organised as follows:

Chapter 1 outlines why SMEs need to adopt a digital mindset to embark on a digital transformation journey. Four necessary mindset shifts are suggested as follows: *Disrupt or be Disrupted, Redefine the Business Strategy, Establish an Agile and Experimentation Mindset* and *Be Data-driven and Exploit Business Areas that cannot be Digitized*. Moreover, one key phenomenon that SMEs cannot ignore in their digital transformation journey is the rise of data analytics and how SMEs can embrace data analytics to improve business productivity and profitability.

While the COVID-19 pandemic has presented numerous challenges for SMEs in different sectors, it also presents collaboration opportunities for SMEs with other organisations (including universities) in their digital transformation journey. Chapter 2 explores some of these collaborative ideas, such as for the food vendors in the food and beverage industry to collaborate with banks to alleviate their pain points in inventory management, payment system, and rental management. Another avenue for collaboration is in the fast-moving consumer goods (FMCG), where companies can collaborate with start-ups providing electronic commerce (e-commerce) intelligence services to better understand customer preferences and spending pattern.

Meanwhile, Chapter 3 offers some thoughts on the benefits that SMEs can reap by engaging students through a university–industry consulting programme. Being involved in such programme will not only strengthen the SME's digital transformation capabilities but also fosters good relationships with the universities and the students (who may be the potential employees of the SMEs). At the same time, by working on real projects with the SMEs, students can equip themselves with digital literacy as well as cultural intelligence, two skillsets that are highly relevant for them to excel in the future workplace.

Chapter 4 serves to provide a guide for SMEs to steer their way through the sometimes-intimidating concept of Artificial Intelligence and Data Analytics (AIDA) and how to practically integrate it into their business. Choosing to adopt AIDA first requires SMEs to gain a clear understanding of what AIDA can do and their enablers. After which, it is also necessary to consider AIDA's impacts on the various aspects of the business and then taking first steps to adoption through basic analytics, while being guided by useful frameworks and models. Only when SMEs have attained a suitable level of data maturity, whereby they have sufficient technical expertise among their ranks, should they then look into using machine learning (ML) to continue the next phase of their AIDA adoption journey.

The subsequent chapters outline the digital transformation efforts in several industries. Accounting organisations are vital components of the economy and Chapter 5 discusses how accounting organisations can approach digital transformation from three key aspects: the role of data analytics is reshaping the work of accountants, how technological advances have led to the emergence of continuous auditing and forensic accounting.

Chapter 6 highlights how digital transformation has reshaped a specific sector in the economy — healthcare. In particular, the COVID-19 pandemic has shown that the future of healthcare is digital! This chapter further examines the trends in modern healthcare landscape, such as the emergence of telehealth and on-demand healthcare, wearable technology, big data, and virtual reality. More importantly, for many Healthcare SME owners, the ultimate question will be as follows: How can SMEs strengthen their digital capability?

Chapter 7 presents the case study of XDel Singapore Pte Ltd, a logistics SME based in Singapore, and how the company is able to pivot itself to embrace the challenging uncertainty as well as the opportunities due to the COVID-19 pandemic. One main reason for its optimism lies in its competitive advantage of being at the forefront of technology through strategic investments in digital technologies. These investments have reaped rewards as the company made good use of data analytics in making important decisions related to route planning, job allocation, and improvement in customer service.

Chapter 8 deals with the case study of Daung Capital, a microfinance SME based in Myanmar. Daung had grown in the past two years to expand its business to reach thousands of low-income customers in Myanmar. In 2019, Daung was launching a new service: a microfinance loan scheme for farmers in rural Myanmar which was one of a kind in the market. This case highlights the various constraints around which the loan product for farmers needed to be constructed. This included a careful credit risk assessment of the target customer base, which was a critical criterion in designing the product.

Information technology is expected to enhance transparency, accuracy, and the communication of financial information as well as offer opportunities for accountants to create value, perform more in-depth analyses, and provide timely financial advice. Chapter 9 focuses on the specific analytical techniques that accountants need to possess to approach and solve common problems faced in the accounting and finance settings: (i) optimisation and (ii) simulation. These digital skillsets will allow them to be proficient with such analysis techniques. Finally, Chapter 10 highlights two initiatives introduced by Singapore Management University's School of Accountancy to equip accounting students with relevant technology skillsets to be future-ready and help SMEs in their digital transformation journey.

1

Accelerating Business Transformation in the Digital Age

Background

Business Transformation involves making fundamental changes in how business is conducted in order to help cope with shifts in market environment. This chapter focuses on the role played by digital technology in business transformation and the mindset shifts required to embark on a digital transformation journey. More relevantly, this chapter also highlights how data analytics is driving digital transformation.

Role of Digital Technology

In the journey of business transformation, digital technology usually plays a catalyst role in accelerating change throughout the organisation, often with an aim of strengthening the value proposition of existing business. A good example is Grab Taxi's on-demand model whose value propositions centre on convenience and immediacy that offer instant access to customers. Another example is Knorex Pte Ltd, which offers analytics services to enable its clients to make sense of their data for better intelligence. Knorex uses an advanced image recognition technique to enhance physical media such as newspapers with interactive contents. Users can point their smart devices at the newspaper article to interact with the embedded contents, such as multimedia, social media sharing and 3D models. These interactive features are embedded with comprehensive tracking to provide analytics to marketers. In this way, marketers can better understand the interest of the readers based on their engagement with the interactive contents.

An infamous example of how digital technology has decimated companies that could not keep up is Kodak. In its heyday in the 1990s, Kodak was the market leader in cameras and films. Yet in 2012, Kodak filed for bankruptcy protection. This rapid decline of Kodak is surprising to many as the company invented digital camera. But over time, the company was focused mainly on its film development and photo printing business. Kodak had missed the boat when digital cameras were incorporated into mobile phones as it reacted too slowly in the digital revolution.

Kodak's case offers an important lesson. In this digital era, companies need to act swiftly to develop a digital strategy, shift organisational structures and remove the barriers that are keeping the organisation from maximising the impact of new digital technologies. After all, if planned and executed well, there is a great opportunity for digital technologies to reframe business and industry models in a significant manner. This may create positive values for consumers, companies and communities.

An important step in technology-driven business transformation is that SMEs must embrace a culture of digitalisation in their processes. For example, top-level commitment in digitalisation is vital to engendering commitment from others. Probably the most important factor in building a culture of digitalisation at small and medium-sized enterprises (SMEs) is having a strong leader, such as the business owner, who is a proponent of digital transformation.

Another important consideration for SMEs is to put in place at every level leaders who are committed to using digital technologies to improve their processes and decision-making. A good example is to establish an effective data management system. It may not necessarily mean owning sophisticated database software, but at least a systematic way of managing data in normal computer set-ups. It is difficult to conduct decision support if you do not have reliable data. Besides the database system, SMEs must provide an open working environment. Employees must be willing to share data and information because they believe their colleagues are going to help them to improve their work, rather than simply turning them away.

Adopting a Digital Mindset

To embark on a digital transformation journey, SMEs may require a significant mindset shift. Once the SME is able to shift the mindset, it is on its way to thriving from just surviving. The capability to disrupt is quickly becoming a competitive advantage for companies. Here, we suggest four necessary mindset shifts in a digital transformation journey: *Disrupt or be Disrupted, Redefine the Business Strategy, Establish an Agile and Experimentation Mindset* and *Be Data-driven and Exploit Business Areas that cannot be Digitised.*

Mindset shift #1: Disrupt or be disrupted

The major cause of disruption is the rapid advancement of technology, which allows new business models to be introduced at an ever-increasing rate and with rapidly declining costs. Addressing this uncertain environment requires disruptive thinking, a willingness to change and reject tried-and-tested ways of creating value. Essentially, SMEs need to be willing to disrupt themselves before others do it to them. This mindset shift requires overcoming the fear that a new product or channel will cannibalise an existing business. Many SMEs struggle with legacy assets and productivity gaps in their own operations and, therefore, find it difficult to overcome the inertia to change. A good example of how a traditional business is embracing digital technologies and transforming its way of doing business is the furniture industry.

In recent years, the furniture industry has undergone significant transformation. Internet furniture sale platforms have replaced many brick-and-mortar stores. Consumers' behaviours have also changed: small orders and purchased on impulse instead of large ticket items, meticulously curated into a home with precision. As a consequence, furniture suppliers also had to react to the change by having production and supply chains that could accommodate volatility in sales behaviours.

In addition, the furniture industry has also adopted virtual reality (VR), augmented reality (AR) and Internet of Things in delivering sales and customer service. With VR, users can select from numerous furniture and furnishing options to help them design their homes without having to be physically present in the space that they are fitting out. This enables retailers to shrink their shopfronts and reduce operating costs. Retailers no longer need to limit their offerings to only what they can physically display in their stores. With AR, customers can experience how their home looks and feels with their chosen furniture even before they pay for them.

With Internet of Things, furniture pieces can be attached to network connectivity and intelligent devices to monitor health statistics, regulate temperatures for comfort and provide feedback on furniture-use preferences. For example, an office table that monitors an employee's use and well-being adjusts its height at regular intervals to suit his or her optimal ergonomic position, may raise productivity and prevent health issues that arise as a result of prolonged sitting. The digital age has seen furniture retailers either moving out of their brick-and-mortar models or turning their stores into flagship click-and-mortar showrooms.

Mindset shift #2: Redefine the business strategy

With digital technologies changing the business environment at rapid speed, a fundamental redefinition of business strategy has become a necessity. Revamping business strategy may include venturing into a new market, pushing for major corporate innovation and others. But before an SME takes any action, it should identify existing strengths and capabilities. This is because while establishing a new business model may sidestep the challenges and constraints of the disrupted legacy business, it is, however, difficult to redesign an SME to compete in an entirely new business area. Therefore, emphasizing on existing strengths and extending internal capabilities will be a good starting point for any digital transformation.

Singapore Post is a good example of how a company is in the process of refocusing its core business. In an announcement made in July 2016, the company acknowledged that its domestic mail business was a burning platform that was subjected to the forces of digital disruption. Domestic mail business is facing an accelerated decline as corporate Singapore becomes increasingly digital. The company is transforming its business model to build new source of growth by extending its foundation into e-commerce logistics. According to the company, this is an important and necessary step to ensure that Singapore Post remains sustainable. Redefining the business strategy is not just unique to Singapore Post. Other successful examples include Fujifilm which applied its capability in attaching chemicals to film and made entry into the cosmetics industry. Similarly, IBM also shifted a large part of their business from hardware to services and consulting.

Mindset shift #3: Establish an agile and experimentation mindset

To respond to disruption, SMEs may want to learn from their disruptors and try to emulate the way they think and act. This may mean SMEs will have to adapt and embrace an agile and experimentation mindset. It is important to create a culture of experimentation where assumptions and iterating concepts are constantly tested. It is fine to experiment and fail. By learning from lessons of failure and applying them to product development, SMEs can continue to innovate so as to ensure each new version of the product better addresses the needs of customers.

To cultivate such a mindset, creating a right culture is important. Rather than specifying desired outcomes, start with a business benefit the company aspires to deliver and let employees work out the best way of achieving it. The mindset ought to be applied across the business units and be supported by the CEO of the SME.

The banking industry is a good role model in creating and cultivating an agile and experimentation mindset. In today's digital age, banks have witnessed an array of new digital solutions and concepts that are coming onto the market. Banks are taking rapid and appropriate actions to innovate and digitise their services. For instance, banks have been primarily dependent upon their branches for their interactions with their customers. They now need to delve much more deeply into how that physical distribution network can be integrated into the whole digital transformation process. Some banks are in the process of coming up with a sound strategy to leverage their physical branches and automated teller machines (ATMs) to enable better digital processes than the fintech, which don't really have a physical presence.

Some banks, however, have already made significant steps in reducing their physical footprint. They have introduced new customer experiences by launching new brands and digital capabilities. For example, banks are beginning to offer many more services through mobile phones so that phones can be used for services beyond checking bank balances and transferring money. Others are rethinking their physical network differently, exploring ways of using a bank branch in a more innovative or value-adding manner. After all, it can be seen as an asset their competitors do not have.

Similarly, the Monetary Authority of Singapore is embracing new technologies, taking advantage of fintech's potential, and reaching out to tech start-ups.[1] It has set up a regulatory sandbox for fintech start-ups to play in without risking customers' data (and money). In addition, it has launched an innovation lab, "Looking Glass", to experiment with fintech solutions and provide consultation to start-ups. The latest notable development is the use of blockchain to enable cross-border payments between major banks. This could be a major step toward legitimising the technology which may bring on board more innovative banking applications.

Mindset shift #4: Be data-driven and exploit business areas that cannot be digitised

Increasingly, companies are utilising big data, coupled with advanced analytics, to improve customer engagement, optimise business processes and point to new monetisation opportunities. Business insights are gleaned when statistics, predictive analytics and data mining are used to inform business processes and improve performance. Companies can do so by identifying data relevant to key business processes and decomposing each process into its supporting decisions, questions and data sources. The end goal is to have a data-driven company where every person has access to data when they need it so as to make better decisions. Being data-driven is about giving business decision makers the power to explore data independently, even if they're working with big or disparate data sources. They need to be able to ask questions and receive answers that are based on data before the decision is actually made. A good example of how data have played an important role in its business processes and decision-making is Singapore's real estate industry.

---

[1] https://www.techinasia.com/mas-fintech-festival-week-2016.

Digitalisation has disrupted the traditional way of doing business and the real estate industry is no exception.[2] For instance, Ohmyhome is a property mobile app created by property agents. Through the app, these property agents reinvented themselves by developing innovative ideas that address the 'inefficiencies' in the market and find new niche markets to tap into. It made real estate information more readily available to consumers and cut down transaction costs.

For property agents whose business has been disrupted by such apps, they may want to focus on business areas that digital technologies cannot address, in order to compete in the market. These underexplored property-related areas include the ageing population, physically disabled people and the green industry. For instance, for the physically disabled people, the real estate apps have not done much to cater to their needs. As the real estate industry continues to be disrupted by technological advancement, the role of a property agent will evolve. As such, property agents will have to quickly adapt and provide value-added services that are beyond what an app can do.

Digital Transformation of SMEs: How Analytics is Driving the Change

Global businesses of every size and in every sector are facing increasing complexity and market volatility. As such, SMEs cannot avoid digital transformation to remain competitive. As they digitise, data begin taking a more important role as feedback. Without it, transformation is limited. Almost all business functions are turning to data-driven analytics and insights as a means to manage this increasing uncertainty and pursue growth through a better understanding of their organisations' customer bases. Responding to consumers' demand, many SMEs are already using a variety of tools to support and track customers, manage social media and run advertising campaigns.

Analytics can draw on, aggregate and analyse data from marketing, sales, and customer service, and derive transformational insights into

---

[2] https://sg.finance.yahoo.com/news/ohmyhome-continues-to-chip-away-at-the-traditional-housing-transaction-process-025503239.html.

customer behaviour and preferences. Big data, for example, is not all about having unlimited amounts of information. It's more a case of receiving high quality, timely information that is specific, relevant and valuable to the business. Putting analytics to work becomes easier all the time and with new generation analytics tools integrating with third parties, hence making the job of a data scientist or business owner far easier, as the hard work of pulling all the data from disparate systems is done on their behalf. The advancement in analytical tools certainly plays a key role in supporting data visualisation, statistical analysis and text mining among other capabilities. For example, an SME can analyse incoming data, such as sales records, marketing patterns, and growth metrics of the company among other things, and creates dashboards for an easier visualisation of the trends. It may also analyse performance metrics such as resource productivity, debt recovery and inventory turnover, which allows the organisation to gain insights into its businesses and integrate business processes as part of a broader enterprise transformation.

Data analytics may also tap on both structured and unstructured data to obtain significant insights. So far, SMEs have relied mainly on structured data. Nevertheless, structured data apparently cover only 20% of the data held in SMEs' computer systems. Approximately 80% of a company's data are stored in an unstructured form which does not lend itself to conventional analysis. These unstructured data may include employees' electronic mails, telephone conversations and many others. So, it may be wise for SMEs to integrate available structured and unstructured data, and then perform data analytics on both types of data that will offer deeper business insights. For a start, it may be useful to create a central repository of a company's data from various sources, such as Excel/CSV, relational and non-SQL databases like Salesforce.

Here are four key steps on how SMEs may embrace data analytics to improve business productivity and profitability.

1. **Defining the Objectives**: The first question is what does the organisation want to achieve from its data? For instance, an organisation may examine whether it can deal with a customer's request quickly and efficiently, hence ensuring customer satisfaction is high. This may have

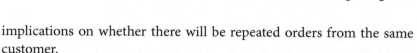

implications on whether there will be repeated orders from the same customer.

2. **Identify all Sources of Data**: Most SMEs will have data stored in a range of isolated areas. The key is to work with what they have and then integrate various data. Besides customer contact information, a business will have additional information that encompasses many different ways it communicates with its customers. For example, the telephony system tracks all calls made and received. Besides call recordings, email records and social media account for further data on communication with customers.

3. **Integrate Data and Consolidate**: The next step is to integrate and consolidate all sources of information within a single tool. If a customer relationship management (CRM) system is unavailable, the SME may need an alternative repository in the cloud that could tap into various databases and systems to present the information in a web-based dashboard for interpretation.

4. **Analyse Dashboards and Turn Data into Actionable Insights**: The combined data on the dashboard should display key performance indicators based on the communication data gathered, such as customer details, their last orders, any previous email communication, when they last called, and who handled the call. Call recordings enable users to hear what was discussed in conversation with customers. This helps SMEs to predict customer behaviour and improve their service before they encounter a complaint. Being predictive is how you can excel in customer service and improve processes. Over time, staff can then be more productive and effective, hence improving revenue and profitability.

Conclusion

In this digital age, SMEs will have to invest in new skills and think hard about how they want to restructure the way they work. That means they will have to become advocates for change and not just passive users of tools and software. The benefits of being digital may be substantial — as indicated by various examples raised in this chapter. However, the deep shift from 'looking digital' to 'being digital' is predicated on intentional efforts to employ these new tools in new ways, to develop and deploy the right talents and to drive new management mindsets. Therein lies the challenge of the leaders: to recognise a deep shift is necessary and to start building the foundation for it.

We expect the future to be one of varied and increasingly ambitious disruption in business, driven by continuous technological innovation. This innovation will drive valuable customer insights, enable the development of new products and services, transform systems and processes to dramatically reduce costs, and enable SMEs that are ready for it to be increasingly agile and able to respond to digital disruption.

The materials for this chapter were adapted from several articles: "Fostering an Analytics Culture", first published on 8 January 2013 by the Business Times; "Using Data Analytics to Raise Productivity and Profitability: 4 Key Steps for SMEs", first published on 20 March 2018 by the Business Times; "How Data Analytics May Turn SMEs into Smart Enterprises", first published on 20 March 2018 by the Business Times; and "Digital Innovation: A Catalyst and Enabler of Achieving Business Sustainability", in the book "Embracing Digital Transformation in Accounting and Finance", CPA Australia, September 2021.

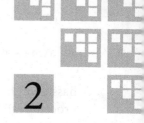

2

Opportunities for Digital Transformation Amid the COVID-19 Pandemic

Background

The COVID-19 pandemic has brought about disruptions in all sectors of the economy. With lockdown being implemented in most of the countries around the world, it has necessitated changes in the business models of small and medium-sized enterprises (SMEs). A glaring area of business opportunity focuses on online business. For instance, retailers who do not yet have an online presence or have not been paying much attention to conducting sales online were caught off-guard during the circuit breaker period which has resulted in decreased footfall and plummeting sales in most physical stores. Therefore, having an online retail presence has become critical for businesses, as they can no longer continue business as usual. This chapter illustrates two case studies on how SMEs can collaborate with other organisations (such as banks and start-ups providing e-commerce intelligence services) in their digital transformation journey.

Part 1: How Can SMEs Take the Opportunities to Collaborate with Banks?

While the current pandemic situation poses challenges to the institutions and SMEs themselves, other organisations (such as banks) view this as new business opportunities to expand their digitalisation efforts in widening clientele base and network and to create customer stickiness. By expanding the suite of service offerings online, clients of banks may now avoid the hassle of having to navigate through various manual processes and procedures, resulting in quicker service times and reduced human errors.

Established in 1941, Bank OCBC NISP is a publicly listed bank in Indonesia, headquartered in Jakarta. OCBC NISP is now actively supporting the digital transformation strategies of SMEs in Indonesia across its corporate banking segment. Meanwhile, it is also pushing for wide adoption of mobile banking platforms across its retail banking segments.

Pain points faced by SMEs in the F&B industry

Cash has long dominated the way of payment in Indonesia, consisting 76% of the whole population. In comparison, cashless payment only contributes percent of the whole population. A low bank penetration is one of the leading factors that is attributed to the low percentage of cashless payments. The over-reliance on cash payment is worrying as cash handling during the still-ongoing COVID-19 pandemic is inadvisable owing to the risk of further transmission of the disease. As a consequence, Bank Indonesia has recently announced to relax rules on credit cards ownership to boost cashless transactions and fuel economic activities amidst the COVID-19 pandemic.

At times like this, though it is unfortunate that offline businesses are disrupted during the COVID-19 pandemic, the convenience and accessibility of online purchases have converted many offline shoppers to online. Coupled with the fact that there is an increasing trend of Internet users and smartphone penetration in Indonesia, businesses have to adapt to the situation and market trends to satisfy market demand. This essentially calls for further development of digital tools and cashless payment to promote purchase convenience not only at unprecedented times like COVID-19 but also for future prospects and sustainability of SMEs.

The evolving technology has contributed significantly to ease people's lives due to its convenience, which is shown by the increasing rates of digital adoption. Therefore, one potential way that the bank can exploit is by integrating seamless adoption of technology from the retailers' perspective.

The solution predominantly targets food vendors as the food and beverages sector could be a prospective and safe area of investment, given the large market in Indonesia. To create stickiness with the bank's potential customers, this solution aims to resolve the pain points of food vendors to achieve efficiency and effectiveness in their business operations, through a smart-retailer application interface. Specifically, the application is an all-in-one dashboard that will display the insights of the business's cash flow and projections to provide comprehensive financial visibility to vendors and serves as a one-stop shop for their business needs.

One of the most critical and yet essential tasks for food vendors is inventory management. Food vendors often find it difficult to control the total cost of inventory efficiently and effectively. To ease the manual monitoring of inventory by the food vendors, the dashboard provides a procurement supply service that tracks the business's inventory levels. The reordering system also adopts a just-in-time methodology that analyses the purchasing behaviour of the food vendor, taking into account their buying patterns and seasonal demand. Automated payment schedules are also calibrated within the application and payments are transferred directly to their suppliers. Additionally, contracts with the suppliers are also consolidated and digitalised, hence, providing an overview for the food vendors and aiding in their decision-making for recontracting.

Rental costs represent one of the biggest cost drivers for food vendors. Flexible payment schemes and more effective management of rental payments could provide the vendors with the cash flows to tide through difficult times. Therefore, the second feature of the dashboard is a rental management system that maintains the food vendors' lease. With the details of the lease, the application helps manage the rental payments and anticipate late payments based on the food vendors' financials.

The availability of a Point-of-Sale (POS) system or other devices to track transactions can help facilitate a cashless solution. This will allow food vendors to track their transactions and generate detailed sales reports which provide insights into their products. Vendors can better understand consumers' preferences and create better products or better manage supplies. The POS system will also provide a comprehensive analysis of their cash flows and working capital.

Finally, to ensure that food vendors are able to continue business operations and protect their bottom line in the event of the unexpected, the application offers the opportunity for companies to ensure their businesses against unforeseeable events that could threaten the well-being of their business.

Benefits of the collaboration

The recommended application targets three main areas (inventory management, payment system and rental management) within the retail food vendor's financial supply chain, which enables the bank to penetrate and manage finances at those various points via the features elaborated earlier. With this level of penetration, it allows the bank to be vertically integrated to create supply chain stickiness in both upstream and downstream. More importantly, cash flow trends can be derived and translated in the form of big data, hence allowing the bank to further develop and tailor financial products that are better suited to this niche financial supply chain.

The current COVID-19 pandemic highlights the important and necessary shift towards contactless payment. Features of the proposed application, such as the online onboarding of customers, contactless payments, robo-advisors for financial projections and data analytics, will reduce the need for human contact via a customer service representative or a financial advisor. This creates a safer business environment for not just customers but also OCBC NISP employees as well.

The shift in consumer patterns and behaviour has created an opportunity for OCBC NISP to capitalise on expanding its digitalisation effort of SMEs in Indonesia. By developing an all-in-one application, it serves as a platform to tackle some of the problems and inconveniences faced by retailers or suppliers while taking into account the shift in consumer behaviour. This will allow OCBC NISP to generate new revenue streams and create customer stickiness through the proposed application.

Part 2: Transforming Businesses with E-commerce Intelligence

2020 had been an extraordinary year as the COVID-19 pandemic struck almost all countries in the world and created an extraordinary impact on businesses worldwide. Singapore and many other Southeast Asian countries were not spared and had to implement lockdowns swiftly. To cope with physical store closures, and the increased volume of online transactions, most businesses tried to revamp their business models and set up online stores to capitalise on the rise of the e-commerce wave.

With the growing trend of online transactions, it has become imperative for companies operating in the Fast Moving Consumer Goods (FMCG) industry to track the performance of their brands on the various online platforms. This need has led to the emergence of E-commerce Intelligence (EI) — a new category of software that enables brand managers to keep track of their stocks and sales in the online space. Over the past year, many start-ups offering data analytics and EI services have emerged and caught the attention of investors and venture capitalists, who are injecting funds to further fuel growth in this sector.[1]

The Growing Need for EI Solutions

EI software relies on machine learning technologies and offers user-friendly and personalised dashboards for managers to make better-informed decisions about their products, which could then lead to increased sales and profits. EI matters because, in today's environment, all companies are focused on being customer-oriented, especially when it comes to online shopping. Having the knowledge of customer preferences and spending patterns at their fingertips enables brand managers in the FMCG industry to implement strategies to drive sales and conversion rates.

---

[1] Taylor Soper, "E-Commerce Intelligence Platform Stackline Raises $50M from Goldman Sachs as Online Retail Booms", Geek Wire, November 20, 2020.

For fledgling EI solution providers, Southeast Asia offers a promising market. In this article, we discuss why this is so and elaborate on the market segments they should focus on to sharpen their competitive edge. We draw insights based on our field research, which includes a case study of an EI solution provider, Digital Commerce Intelligence Pte Ltd (DCI). Our analysis helps make sense of the demand for EI applications from FMCG firms based in Singapore and, more broadly, in Southeast Asia. We highlight that EI solution providers should build their data storytelling capability as a strategy to differentiate themselves from their competitors.

The projected growth for the e-commerce sector suggests that prospects are good for EI solution providers. In 2020, over two billion e-commerce customers worldwide pushed total retail commerce sales to reach US$4.28 trillion, and it is projected that e-commerce transactions will account for 21.8% of total global retail sales by 2024.[2] In Southeast Asia, the e-commerce sector has grown by an impressive 35% last year and is expected to grow by another 14% to reach US$45 billion this year.[3] There is a myriad of reasons for the continued growth of online retail. These include an overall increase in disposable income, the convenience of online shopping, and various marketing strategies, such as promotions and free shipping or delivery above a certain price point. The rise in transaction volume is also due to higher mobile phone and Internet penetration rates across several developing economies particularly in Southeast Asia.[4] Additionally, retail powerhouses like Walmart and Uniqlo are increasingly enhancing their presence online, thereby driving e-commerce demand and sales.[5]

---

[2] David Coppola, "E-commerce Worldwide — Statistics & Facts", Statista, July 14, 2021.

[3] Ethan Cramer-Flood, "Southeast Asia Ecommerce 2021: Public Health Uncertainty Clouds Outlook", Insider Intelligence, July 6, 2021.

[4] Bain & Company, "e-Conomy SEA 2020 — Resilient and Racing Ahead: Southeast Asia at Full Velocity", 2020.

[5] Eric Ng, "Uniqlo Parent Fast Retailing to Strengthen Online Sales after Beating Retail Gloom to Report Better-than-Expected First-Half Profit", *South China Morning Post*, April 9, 2021.

We expect the market for EI software to continue growing at a rapid rate over the next five years due to two reasons. First, there will be fast-growing demand for e-commerce data analytics in Southeast Asia due to the rising e-commerce transaction volume. Second, the competition between big brands on digital platforms is expected to intensify. This will also increase their demand for and investment in e-commerce data analytics, as they attempt to gain and sustain an information edge over their rivals. The parallel increase in digital marketing solutions budgets will drive market growth for EI solution providers (refer to Figure 1). In fact, we argue that EI solution providers have the potential to gain more market share if they continue to invest in real-time analytical capabilities driven by Artificial Intelligence (AI). Being able to offer prompt, accurate, and rich insights is going to be a key value proposition, given how rapidly sales estimates and ratings move in the e-commerce sphere.

Changes in Digital versus Traditional Marketing Spend

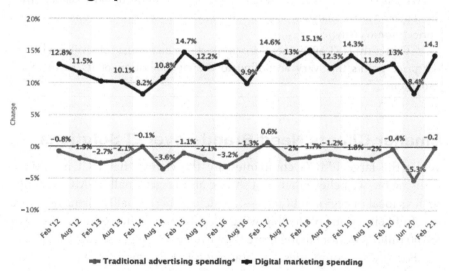

Figure 1.   Trends on traditional marketing spend and digital marketing spend
Source: A. Guttmann, "Change in Digital Marketing Spending and Traditional Advertising according to CMOs in the United States from 2012 to 2020", Statista, February 2021.

Digital Commerce Intelligence Pte Ltd

Compared to larger markets like the US and China, accessibility to market performance data for retailer brands on e-commerce platforms in Southeast Asia like Lazada and Shopee is limited and fragmented. To address this gap, Digital Commerce Intelligence Pte Ltd (DCI), a start-up based in Singapore, built solutions that use advanced data science techniques and AI to provide e-commerce market performance insights and competitive intelligence for consumer goods brands and retailers in Southeast Asia.

DCI currently offers two types of data service offerings to its customers. The first offering is a brand-level key performance indicator (KPI) monitoring tool that consolidates and analyses digital shelf data, turning it into insights and actionable recommendations. This *Brand-Level Tracker* offers real-time monitoring of vital KPIs, stock availability, pricing compliance across all stores, and customer ratings and reviews.

The second offering is an e-commerce category-level competitive intelligence dashboard that gives its customers a holistic view of their market size and potential, allowing them to identify areas of improvement. A *Market-Level Tracker*, it offers features like weekly data refresh, brand category size and market share analytics, sales trends analytics, brand portfolio analytics and price/promo analytics.

Currently, DCI offers these two products on an annual subscription basis at price points that vary according to the customisation of its customers' solutions.

Smaller Clients Need Brand-Level EI Solutions

While the large FMCG companies are the clients that DCI is initially focusing on, we believe that DCI should also target smaller FMCG clients, such as local or regional brands — we define these smaller clients as those that fulfil either one of the following conditions: revenue of not more than S$100 million or not having more than five best-selling product categories.

For these companies, a brand-level KPI monitoring tool that consolidates and provides an analysis of digital shelf data, turning them into insights and actionable recommendations, would be an appropriate product. Digital shelf data comprise retail data, such as inventory availability. In turn, brand-level KPIs based on such digital shelf data can ensure that the company's products do not go out of stock.

As an example, using this digital shelf data, an FMCG company based in Asia selling beer in the e-commerce space can compare the performance of its product with respect to that of other beers (e.g., Tiger, Heineken, and Guinness) on e-commerce platforms, such as Lazada. The company can then take appropriate actions, such as stocking up more beers on weekends to attract more consumers to buy its products.

In our field research, a small FMCG firm shared that while a category-level competitive intelligence dashboard would be useful, it was unable to afford the product due to budget constraints and its small scale. However, it found the brand-level monitoring tool to be more useful at its current business stage. It too had been experiencing excess inventory due to the difficulty of coordinating sales and inventory across its retail, corporate sales, and online channels. This resulted in additional costs from unsold perishable goods and the need to rent warehouse space.

Therefore, the features of a brand-level KPI monitoring tool are more suited to the needs of smaller firms as it is more affordable and can help them achieve greater operational and marketing efficiency. Hence, one recommendation for EI solution providers focusing on smaller players is to build and market brand-level EI software that caters to the latter's needs.

Bigger Players Need a Suite of Solutions

While there is no ready definition yet of larger FMCG players (e.g., Unilever), we argue that they would be companies that easily have 30 or more product categories under many different segments, such as beauty, personal care, and food.

During our field studies, we interviewed three brand managers from multinational FMCG firms to understand their needs for EI software in terms of value and cost. Not surprisingly, larger players with scale and reach find market-level trackers useful. Market-level trackers provide information, such as the market share of a brand in a particular product category (e.g., beer). Additionally, they provide information, such as which beer brands are the top sellers each week. This information helps brand managers decide whether they should offer discounts to boost sales and increase their market share.

For instance, one brand manager affirmed the utility of a category-level competitive intelligence dashboard for e-commerce teams as it provided insights into the competition that were not readily shared by e-retailers. Brand-level trackers were less useful because the existing dashboards provided by e-retailers already allowed brands to analyse their own performance across categories and markets.

A key insight from our interviews was that both market-level trackers (e.g., category-level competitive intelligence dashboards) and brand-level ones (e.g., brand-level KPI monitoring tools) were useful but for different reasons. Market-level EI software, such as category-level competitive intelligence dashboards, was more useful for managers in global roles or category managers that require top-line insights into product performance, while brand-level monitoring tools and solutions were more useful for local brand managers, managers directly handling sales, or those in charge of executional strategies. Such brand-level software could also be enriched if EI solution providers added value by incorporating bolt-on features that work side-by-side with the core systems to provide supplementary functionality. One example would be data integration from e-retailer platforms, such as Lazada and Shopee so that local brand managers can track whether their performance is better or worse than their competitors on these platforms.

EI solution providers that target larger players should, therefore, consider the prospects of cross-selling both types of EI software that cater to the needs of different teams in large FMCG firms.

Data Storytelling: A Compelling Must-Have

According to technology consulting firm Forrester, satisfaction with analytics dipped 21% between 2014 and 2015 despite investments in big data.[6] While 74% of firms want to be data-driven, only 29% are confident of connecting analytics to action. This presents a gap in the market that

---

[6] Brian Hopkins, "Think You Want to be 'Data-Driven'? Insight Is the New Data", Forrester, March 9, 2016.

is still largely unexplored and open for EI solution providers to exploit in order to offer better value to their clients, and fulfil their need for fast and actionable intelligent insights.

A prominent value proposition based on identified customers' needs would be to offer packaged data that catered to specific job scopes for customers to gain easily understood, readily accessible, and actionable insights. This could help EI solution providers acquire more customers, especially smaller-scale companies that are looking for cost-effective market intelligence solutions.

We argue that compelling, concise, and convenient data storytelling is one way to address their needs. By presenting only the most relevant and contextualised insights into customers based on their roles and needs through data storytelling, EI solution providers can tap on this opportunity and increase customer satisfaction. In turn, their clients also stand to gain from automated data storytelling enabled by AI, as this feature helps reduce workloads while targeting customer needs better. Data storytelling combines the usage of narrative, visuals, and data to explain, engage, and enlighten customers.[7] A narrative is a vital component of communicating the information and insights that an EI solution firm has to offer. Data storytelling capabilities would facilitate the acquisition of enthusiastic adopters by making a more compelling sales pitch, as potential customers would be able to perceive the immediate value EI solution providers can add to their brands and departments, allowing actionable insights to be communicated more easily within their organisation. When such reports are shared or published, this may even boost "land-and-expand" selling to adjacent cross-functional departments or sister brands.

EI solution providers can also consider using data storytelling tools to deliver automated, customised reports to clients to surface key insights in an effortless, enjoyable, and digestible manner. Telling a compelling story with the data will help customers remember an EI solution provider's products and they are more likely to believe in the value of these products. For instance, in the case of beers, besides presenting the data on the dashboards, the data storytelling solutions can compile the data into a

---

[7] Brent Dykes, "10 Ways to Make Your Dashboards More Actionable", Forbes, September 12, 2019.

report that shows the sales of the company's brand with respect to all other beer brands in a week. Additionally, the data could provide interactive stories that show the brand managers what they could change to achieve their desired sales target.

EI solution providers could consider leveraging technologies like natural language generation (NLG), deep learning, and augmented analytics to implement data storytelling tools. For example, NLG is employed by data storytelling company Narrativa to transform data into human knowledge in real time and offer automated products to allow companies to get an immediate response to make data-driven decisions in a timely manner. By blending e-commerce intelligence with data storytelling capabilities that NLG provides, EI solution firms can automate some of the resource-intensive after-sales services they provide on an *ad hoc* basis for their clients, such as data exploration and analysis, and report generation. This would also enable these firms to scale successfully by acquiring more customers without hiring more consultants and data analysts.

There are three possible methods to implement such data storytelling products. First, an EI solution provider could act as a middleman and purchase contracts from data storytelling companies for its clients. It also has the option to develop the solution in-house. Alternatively, it could explore potential partnerships or collaborations with data storytelling start-ups.

Based on our estimates, the implementation of self-developed data storytelling products or adoption of the middleman role will not be financially feasible for a start-up like DCI. The contribution margin ratio for a bundled package of a category-level competitive intelligence dashboard and an additional data storytelling tool will be very low, due to the high fixed costs involved in either of the first two options, which will result in a much higher break-even figure. Therefore, we recommend that new and smaller EI solution providers should seek other start-ups that provide such services. This way, both parties stand to benefit from mutual collaboration. A successful partnership would allow both companies to gain greater reach and publicity, thus freeing up resources to focus on their own specialty technology and grow their client bases.

Conclusion

The Southeast Asia market for EI solutions is still in its nascent stage. This implies that the market is not only fragmented but also lacks clear standardisation across the industries. Players are offering variations of the same service. At the same time, customers too have not formed a finalised, complete idea of the products that they are looking for. While having no clear industry leader in this early development stage can be beneficial for fledging providers like DCI, it also means that they must communicate clearly and constantly with potential clients to refine their value propositions and product offerings in order to capture a larger market share.

Within the FMCG space, EI solution providers have a good chance of capturing the growing market. They just have to be clear about which market segment (i.e., local, regional, or global players) to target with which blend of offerings (e.g., brand-level tracker only or a suite of brand and market-level monitoring solutions) and pay attention to data storytelling.

Part 1 of this chapter was first published on 31 December 2020 by the Business Times under the title "Students Can Assimilate Different Cultures via Virtual Learning".

Part 2 of this chapter was first published in November 2021 by Asian Management Insights under the title "Transforming Businesses with E-Commerce Intelligence".

3

Enhancing SMEs' Digital Transformation Capabilities through Partnership with Universities

Background

Apart from collaborations with other organisations as elaborated in the previous chapter, one other way in which small and medium-sized enterprises (SMEs) can enhance their digital transformation capabilities is through partnership with universities. This chapter outlines three benefits that organisations can reap by engaging students through a university–industry consulting programme. Such a programme not only benefits the industry partner but also strengthens the students' digital literacy skills and cultural intelligence, especially if they work together with overseas SMEs.

Part 1: Enhancing SMEs' Data Analytics Capability

Harnessing the power of data analytics, SMEs can now generate visualisations of the company's historical data to date and predictions for the future — something which is nearly impossible before the era of big data. For example, an SME can analyse incoming data, such as sales records, marketing patterns, and growth metrics of the company, and create dashboards for easier visualisation of the trends. The company can also deploy data analytics to support the making of critical business decisions that include new product development, investigation of supplier or production issues, formulation of product pricing and promotion strategies.

While most would agree that data analytics could bring significant benefits to SMEs, nevertheless, many SMEs are still relying on ballpark estimates to make key strategic decisions rather than hard data from scientific calculations. A major obstacle for SMEs is that many are still operating as traditional, non-digital businesses, and they perceive data analytics as "mumbo jumbo". Due to lack of knowledge, many SME business owners also feel intimidated adopting data analytics practices. They simply do not know how they could leverage their existing data to make better decisions. Furthermore, there is also this issue of having a lower priority of allocating budgets for long-term planning and data analysis.

An SME–university partnership model

To overcome the adoption challenge, SMEs could consider enhancing their data analytics capability by partnering universities through faculty mentored student projects. SMEs may benefit significantly from such a partnership. These benefits could include additional manpower for value-added projects; faculty-guided consultancy; potential new hires who are exposed to the industry and have the knowledge of the company; exchange knowledge with faculty and students; innovative solutions from millennials; and examine exploratory projects which may be overlooked given day-to-day responsibilities. The collaboration will also allow university students to better understand the growing complexities in running an SME and build business capabilities that will benefit the overall SME sector. One such partnership that has worked well so far is the collaboration between SMEs and Singapore Management University (SMU) through its SMU-X initiative, launched in 2015. The SMU-X initiative offers an experiential curriculum that motivates students, to apply their knowledge in solving real-world problems with mentorship by professors and industry partners.

Using Accounting as an example, since 2015, several SMEs have taken up the opportunity to collaborate with SMU School of Accountancy in one of its courses — Accounting Analytics Capstone. The capstone course is one that all SMU students that undertake the 2nd major in Accounting Data and Analytics take in their final year. The hands-on capstone project represents an opportunity for students to apply what they have learnt in the accounting data and analytics curriculum, into helping SMEs to solve complex financial analytical problems in real-world setting.

Projects completed in the Accounting Analytics Capstone course include the following: developing Excel/Tableau dashboards for financial performance evaluation, inventory planning, and payment and collection cycles reviews; constructing revenue and cash flow predictive modelling; conducting simulation of business scenarios on customer demand and inventory control; developing a balanced scored card encompassing both financial and non-financial performance metrics; exploring impacts of block chain technology and artificial intelligence on the effectiveness of audit design process.

Case study: A food manufacturer in Singapore

An SME from the food manufacturing industry in Singapore commissioned a team of five accounting students from the Accounting Analytics Capstone course, offered by the School of Accountancy of SMU in January 2018 to build a financial forecasting model with both analytical and predictive capabilities. The project was subsequently completed in 14 weeks.

The food manufacturer had been keeping track of more than 40 varieties of food products in different packaging designs and weight. In addition to the various retail packaging formats were the customisations for private labelling, again in different packaging, weight, and quantity for different customers, hence resulting in too many stock keeping units (SKUs) to manage, and the problem of holding too much raw materials and packaging materials.

Another issue for the food manufacturer was that ideas of venturing into new and different markets had surfaced before, but they did not materialise. The big deterrence to further global expansion was the absence of important supporting information, such as operating costs, return-on-investment, production quantity, and so on. This information was a must to assess the potential risk of investing in different foreign markets, and its absence ultimately determined the overall expansion strategy. Thus, a key value proposition of data analytics was that it could help the company to visualise what the future holds and, hence, in justifying decisions made.

With the company's historical sales data, the analytical findings revealed seasonal buying patterns by local consumers. It also showed the products which were most responsive during those periods. For instance, a spike in consumer demand was reported during the festive months of December to February every year, which coincided with Christmas, New Year and Chinese New Year celebrations, and which were the most popular food items bought by Singaporeans during this time.

Acting on these patterns, the food manufacturer could now manage the supply chain process more efficiently during the festive period by adjusting the procurement of raw materials, and managing production, marketing, distribution and warehousing suitably to cater to the increased demand.

Using predictive analytics, the company could calculate the likelihood of success when introducing a new product in a new market. The predictive model suggested a few countries that had market potential for the specific food item consumption, and based on the preferred manufacturing quantity, it would also calculate the start-up costs, the sales volume that would enable the company to breakeven, the return-on-investment and the expected profit following five years of operations. The predictive model also helped quantify the potential reduction in revenue of well-established products upon market introduction of a new product variant under the same family brand. Throughout the project, the student team had to brainstorm on possible actionable insights and recommendations using the financial model they developed.

Conclusions

Overall, the experience for the SME and SMU was a beneficial one with several takeaways. Through the partnership with universities, SMEs could gain a completely new perspective to some of their problems and sometimes even learnt of a novel and effective solution to an issue. Additionally, they could work with some of the students prior to recruitment visits. We foresee such collaboration between SMEs and universities to grow in the years to come.

Part 2: Developing SMEs' Online Business Strategy

The COVID-19 pandemic has brought about a significant shift in shopping behaviour from offline to online among Singaporean consumers. According to data from data analytics firm Nielsen, 37% of Singaporean consumers have increased online shopping activities since the COVID-19 outbreak. This shift towards online shopping, food delivery and e-groceries may persist beyond the COVID-19 period.

While the increase in online shopping has benefited online stores, many businesses who do not yet have an online presence or have not been paying much attention to conducting sales online were caught off-guard during the circuit breaker period which has resulted in decreased footfall and plummeting sales in most physical stores. For example, it was reported that only 5% of the heartland shops in Singapore can operate digitally ("Heartland Shops' Business Battered by Coronavirus Crisis," *Straits Times*, 7 May 2020). Therefore, having an online retail presence has become critical for businesses, as they can no longer continue business as usual.

To devise an online business strategy, businesses must rethink who their customers are and how they want to serve their customers. This means that they might need to understand and pay more attention to engage "millennials", who are digital natives and are expected to comprise as much as 75% of global workforce by 2025. Millennial customers are known to value experiences, discoveries, and excitement during online shopping. Therefore, businesses may have to put in place a digital experience that involves not only more than just providing customer service online but also using social media and technology in ways that create delightful experiences across all touchpoints — from design to content to customer support to creating a seamless offline-to-online experience. While the idea of engaging millennials seems like common sense, this is no easy feat. A major obstacle for many businesses is that they lack a clear understanding of millennials' shopping behaviours online and, as a result, not knowing how to establish a "millennial-friendly" digital experience to boost their online sales.

An SME–university partnership model

To better understand millennial customers, businesses may consider developing their online business strategy by partnering with universities through faculty-mentored student projects. Such student projects come with no cost to businesses. In addition, businesses may benefit from having additional manpower for value-added projects; faculty-guided consultancy; potential new hires who are exposed to the industry and have knowledge of the company; exchanging knowledge with faculty and students; and most importantly, co-developing innovative digital solutions with millennials who are likely their potential customers. The collaboration will also allow university students to understand the benefits and challenges of running a business. At the same time, the trend towards digital transformation of businesses has given rise to new opportunities for students who may be inspired to become future entrepreneurs by becoming disruptors in the industry themselves.

One such partnership that has worked well so far is the collaboration between businesses and Singapore Management University (SMU) through its SMU-X initiative which was launched in 2015. The SMU-X initiative offers an experiential curriculum that motivates students to apply their knowledge in solving complex real-world problems with mentorship by professors and industry partners. For example, since 2017, several businesses have taken up the opportunity to collaborate with SMU School of Accountancy in one of its courses: Accounting for Entrepreneurship. The course is open to students from any discipline during their four years of study at SMU. Projects completed in the Accounting for Entrepreneurship course include online business strategy; feasibility study of new product and service; developing product prototype; budget forecasting and break-even analysis; product costing; cash flow analysis; and financial/operational performance visualisation dashboard.

Case study: A technology company in Singapore

In January 2019, VV Technology, an AI-driven technology company founded in Singapore, commissioned 72 students (i.e., five to six students per team) from the Accounting for Entrepreneurship course to complete several projects over two academic semesters ending in November 2019.

The company is currently developing online platforms in food delivery, e-commerce, and smart retail to help connect merchants (including those who may not have an online presence) to the significant number of millennials in Singapore and, later, in ASEAN. The projects with SMU aimed to leverage technologies, such as big data, blockchain, cloud and artificial intelligence, to sharpen VV Technology's understanding of the target market of millennials and narrow down the types of products and services that VV Technology is launching in Singapore and ASEAN.

One of the projects focused on food delivery. Students performed background research on companies that were offering online food delivery services in Singapore. With the research and data analyses, students brainstormed possible online business solutions and developed several useful outputs, such as the profile of a delivery rider, the commissions charged by each food delivery platform, and the opportunities that VV Technology could tap on in the competitive online market environment. The value of such research proves to be very important and timely, especially with the increasing prominence of food and grocery delivery platforms during the current COVID-19 pandemic in Singapore and other parts of the world. In addition, students prepared budgets and forecasts, and conducted break-even analysis for several recommended products and services that VV Technology was planning to introduce to the Singapore and ASEAN online marketplaces. Such analyses required students to apply managerial accounting concepts that they learnt in class and come up with practical recommendations.

Through the collaboration, the students learned practical and cognitive skills on how to perform market research and obtained useful findings from the ground through surveys, as well as tested the market feasibility with prototypes while keeping business sustainability in mind. The research and presentations by the students provided beneficial insights into which areas VV Technology should explore and focus for their online business strategy.

Conclusions

Through the partnership with universities, businesses may gain a completely new perspective to some of their problems and sometimes even learn of a novel and effective solution to an issue. During the current COVID-19 pandemic, developing an online business strategy may become a priority for some businesses. By working with university students to devise a "millennial-friendly" online business model, businesses may be able to better exploit business opportunities online. Subsequently, moving beyond the COVID-19 period, businesses may consider working with university students to brainstorm and establish plausible post-crisis recovery business strategies and models. We foresee such beneficial and collegial collaboration between businesses and universities to grow in the years to come.

Part 3: Developing Cultural Intelligence and Digital Literacy via a University's Overseas Student Consulting Programme

Background

According to a recent McKinsey & Company Global Survey of executives, the COVID-19 pandemic has accelerated companies' digital transformation efforts in the way they do business. Particularly, the focus of transformation has been on digitalisation of customer and supply chain interactions and the significant increase of digitally enabled products. The survey results have also confirmed the rapid shift toward interacting with customers through digital channels as these online customers are no longer based only locally but from countries around the world. To stay competitive in this new business environment requires new strategies and practices. As such, there is a pressing need for business executives to adopt a global mindset and enhance their level of digital literacy, as cultural intelligence and digital capability are critical components of new online business models.

With rapid transformation in the accountancy sector, it is, therefore, not difficult to understand why there is a growing demand for advanced digital knowledge and adequate global exposure for accounting professionals. This calls for an urgent injection of digital knowledge and cultural intelligence in the accounting education that would allow students to navigate a future workplace where use of technology and dealing with global clientele are the norm. Therefore, teaching pedagogy at universities has started to evolve from content teaching to engaging students in active learning, hence focusing on applying and reflecting knowledge through project-based learning (PBL). An essential feature of PBL is it is increasingly requiring partnership between universities and companies in devising effective solutions to address complex problems. This section aims to shed light on students' learning experience of cultural intelligence and digital literacy in a PBL programme at the Singapore Management University (SMU).

Overseas study mission course at SMU

Since December 2009, the SMU School of Accountancy has been regularly organising accounting study mission trips to visit companies and organisations in various countries across Asia. The countries visited include China, Hong Kong, Indonesia, Japan, Laos, Thailand, and Vietnam. The trip usually lasts for at least a week and students will get the chance to interact with the business leaders in those countries.

More recently, some of the study mission trips have been converted into SMU-X Overseas (hereafter denoted as SMU-XO) courses since August 2018, which offers an overseas experiential learning opportunity for students. One important objective of the SMU-XO course is to provide students with the learning opportunity to apply the theories and knowledge learnt in classroom into devising practical solutions for real organisations. In addition to visits to companies and organisations, students will also participate in a consultancy project, which is assigned by the project sponsor (typically a company that is based in the country visited).

In addition, one important feature of the SMU-XO pedagogy is that it is a tripartite collaboration between the faculty member (who will be the instructor of the course), the students, and the overseas project sponsor. Through the project collaboration, students will learn how to solve business problems with guidance from the faculty and mentors assigned by the industry partner (i.e., the project sponsor) from problem definition to final presentation, while simultaneously testing their skills in real-world settings.

Overall, a typical SMU-XO course aims to fulfil the following learning objectives: (1) understand the foreign country and its political economic development and socio-political diversity, (2) solve real-world problems through a student consultancy project, (3) incorporate experiential and peer learning, (4) incorporate active mentoring by faculty and project sponsors, and (4) learn how to handle uncertainty in a project. Therefore, the PBL with overseas clients and exposure to foreign culture are expected to broaden students' cultural intelligence and allow them to be more prepared to take on cross-cultural collaboration in the future.

Case study 1: Study mission trip to Laos

The country of focus in the first case study is Laos and the project sponsor is Company A, a prominent Laotian conglomerate with business interests across a range of industries including fast moving consumer goods (FMCG), automotive, agriculture, and construction. The semester commenced in August 2018 and ended in December 2018, with students first attending six seminars in Singapore and then visiting the Laotian cities of Luang Prabang and Vientiane over a period of eight days. 29 SMU undergraduate students enrolled in the course. They were allocated to five project teams and completed three projects.

While in Laos, students visited six organisations, including Company A, to provide them with the opportunity to interact with a range of local representatives and industry practitioners, further enhancing the cross-cultural learning experience. Together with Company A, faculty from SMU scoped the following three projects for the students to undertake throughout the semester:

Project 1: Balanced Scorecard and Dashboard
Company A was looking to improve the tools that they use for comparing and tracking of business performance in their automotive business. Accordingly, students were tasked to develop a balanced scorecard that (i) can be universally applied across automotive sub-units, (ii) make business sense for the company, and (iii) can be practically implemented. They were also tasked to create dashboards to complement the balanced scorecard by allowing Company A to effectively monitor and track business performance.

Project 2: Valuation
Company A was in the early stages of exploring the sale or listing of the branded tires and branded motorcycles sub-units within its automotive business. However, one stumbling block had been the lack of reliable valuations of these sub-units. Accordingly, students were tasked to use

relevant accounting information to develop valuation models to provide relevant insights into Company A in its continuing discussions on a possible sale or listing of the various sub-units.

Project 3: Setting Up of a Holding Company

As a family business, Company A has issues related to corporate governance. To improve corporate governance, Company A is considering setting up a holding company. Students were tasked to examine the various options available to Company A and to provide recommendations that could inform Company A's decision on a possible restructuring of its business to improve its corporate governance.

The project work commenced in August 2018. They were mentored by SMU faculty and consulted frequently (virtually) with senior employees of Company A. They concluded their projects by providing Company A with a final presentation and written report of their final prototypes/models/recommendations during their visit to the premises of Company A in December 2018.

Recommendations to Company A in Laos

Company A's senior management team, including its president, was present to interact with students and listen to their presentations in December 2018.

Balanced scorecard and dashboard: The two project teams assigned to this project came up with comprehensive balanced scorecards that used weighted measures that Company A could use to track its performance from the financial, customer, internal business, and learning and growth perspectives. They also created accompanying dashboards using the Microsoft Excel software that would allow Company A to effectively track the performance measures described in the balanced scorecard. Advanced Excel features, such as macros and "what-if" analysis, were also incorporated into students' dashboards.

Valuation: The two project teams that were assigned to this project developed a range of valuation models to value Company A's sub-units. These models were developed using the Microsoft Excel software and employed techniques including the net asset method, the discounted cash flow method, and the comparable companies method. Advanced Excel features, such as macros, were also incorporated into students' dashboards.

Setting up of holding company: The project team that was assigned to this project thoroughly researched the topic and came up with a suite of insights and recommendations that were relevant to Company A. Their report and presentation highlighted the key issues related to succession planning that were relevant to a large family run company like Company A, outlined the key benefits of setting up a holding company, and examined the options available to Company A in setting up a holding company (including which jurisdiction to set up the holding company, and pros and cons of listing the holding company).

Case study 2: Study mission trip to Indonesia

Meanwhile, the second case study revolves around a "virtual" study mission trip to Indonesia and project collaboration with Bank B, one of the oldest banks in Indonesia. The semester started in January 2020, and it was supposed to culminate in a study trip with a final presentation at the headquarter of Bank B, located in Jakarta, in early May 2020. Twenty eight SMU undergraduate students enrolled in the course. They were allocated to five project teams and completed two projects.

Project 1: Penetrating the Education Industry

Given the large population in Indonesia, Bank B constantly strives to gain more exposure to potential customers in Indonesia and acquire them as its customer base. In the project collaboration with SMU, the problem statement that was given to the students is to explore initiatives in penetrating the education industry to broaden its clientele base and create customer stickiness.

Project 2: Marketing Bank B's corporate Internet banking application

To serve non-individual customers' needs in running their businesses, Bank B through its Cash Management Division has developed a corporate Internet banking application, named Application V, providing access to customers' accounts anytime anywhere. Customers can both view their accounts and transact through the Internet. The main objective of the project is to come up with a marketing plan to increase the usage and penetration rate of Application V.

In the first two weeks of the semester, online Skype calls were made between the students and the mentors assigned by Bank B. The problem statement was clearly explained and defined in the Skype calls and the mentor also addressed some initial questions by the students. After performing their background research, the students did a mid-term presentation in front of the teaching faculties (which includes the instructor and the adjunct teaching mentor) in Week 9 of the semester. Not only did they obtain "live" feedback from the teaching faculties but they were also able to engage the faculties in an interactive discussion which proved to be useful in terms of how they can refine their recommendations. After the presentation, the students continued with the projects for the remaining part of the semester.

Due to the COVID-19 pandemic and border closures, the company visits to Jakarta had to be cancelled and as a result, contingency plans were activated. The company presentations by the business leaders representing the technology, accounting, and start-up sectors were rearranged and done virtually via a teleconferencing platform (WebEx) in the last week of April 2020. More importantly, the faculty and mentors assigned from Bank B also decided for the final presentation to be pre-recorded and presented to the senior management team of Bank B online (also via WebEx), at the end of April 2020.

Recommendations to Bank B in Indonesia

The following recommendations were offered by the students doing the two projects with Bank B, when they presented their work to a group of senior management teams of Bank B in late April 2020.

Penetrating the education industry: One of the proposed recommendations to penetrate the education industry is by integrating seamless adoption of technology from the retailers' perspective. To create stickiness with Bank B's potential customers, the proposed solution by the students aims to resolve the pain points of food vendors in the education industry to achieve efficiency and effectiveness in their business operations. Specifically, the solution is to develop an application that is intended to be a smart retailer-managed application interface and aims to adopt a seamless integrated onboarding for vendors and serve as a one-stop shop for their business needs. An all-in-one dashboard will display the insights of the business's cash flow and projections to provide comprehensive financial visibility for the vendors. There are four main features which tackle the main pain points of retailers and seek to create stickiness by onboarding retailers onto Bank B's ecosystem: inventory management, rental and loan management, payment management and business insurance.

Marketing Bank B's corporate Internet banking application: To market Application V to SMEs, one of the proposed recommendations was to adopt the 3C strategy — Creation of content to promote the application through YouTube and other social media platform; Collaboration with various YouTubers who are also SME owners to review the application as well as provide tutorials regarding the platform; and Continuation through the setting up of a business association to integrate SME clients into the system and increase stickiness while rolling out new initiatives efficiently.

Feedback from Client Partners

The senior management team of both Company A and Bank B praised the students for their professionalism and well-executed projects. Overall, they were pleased with the quality of the recommendations and expressed keen interest in implementing SMU students' respective solutions.

Following the completion of the collaboration with SMU, Company A's president sent a letter of appreciation to the university to record his appreciation of the work that had been done. The letter expressed his gratitude for the "warm partnership and support" extended to his company. It also highlighted that Company A was "impressed by the level of professionalism, the quality work and concerted efforts" that the students had shown. In discussing the benefits that Company A received from sponsoring the projects, Company A's president highlighted that "in today's increasingly competitive market, real-time and objective data are crucial to aid in the business making-decision and identify and grow talents in the company. The projects embarked on by the SMU students exactly helped in these matters and point out the areas Company A needs to improve on to stay competitive in the market. Moreover, these projects also demonstrate the importance of collaboration, which Company A hopes more companies in Laos can consider to embrace."

The Head of Cash Management of Bank B also thanked the students for the excellent effort put in the project collaborations. He further commented that the mentor managers who had been put in charge of those projects would be summarising the presentations to the key stakeholders as he believed that some of the recommendations can be adapted to expand Bank B's business. He also hoped that the project collaboration has enriched SMU students' horizon and mindset, especially when considering banking as a future career possibility.

Feedback from Faculty Members

The faculty members who participated in the two courses also shared that they had gained valuable exposure to the Laotian and Indonesian economies and insights into how universities could collaborate to not only enhance the learning of students but also bring benefits to stakeholders involved in the collaboration. Specifically, the faculty involved in the Laos study mission commented, "The SMU-XO course provided me with a unique opportunity to work with senior executives of one of the most prominent family-run companies in Laos. I gained a first-hand perspective into the unique challenges of doing business in a developing Southeast Asian economy like Laos. Teaching this course also allowed me to gain insights into how academia and industry can work together to bring about unique benefits to various stakeholders."

Meanwhile, the other faculty member in charge of the "virtual" study mission to Indonesia further highlighted the need for agility in terms of immediate response brought about because of the cancellation of the study trip due to the COVID-19 pandemic. The cooperativeness of the project sponsor (Bank B) and their support in terms of accommodating online presentations in front of their senior managers were also very much appreciated.

Feedback from Students

End of course feedback evaluation was conducted for students involved in both courses. Questions were asked on a wide range of aspects of the courses: (i) Clarity of objectives and expectations, (ii) stimulation of interests in content and PBL, (iii) facilitation and mentoring skills, (iv) quality and frequency of feedback, (v) creating opportunities for you to learn from others (partners, guest speakers, and peers), (vi) providing you with the opportunities to understand a different culture/way of working overseas, and (vii) enhancing your understanding of the country's economy and industry. Students were then asked to provide their feedback on a Likert-like scale for the above-mentioned questions on a scale of 1 (Extremely Poor) to 7 (Excellent). The mean score for each question is above that of the University-average score, highlighting that students who participated in both courses had benefitted from the experiential PBL with an overseas client partner.

Other qualitative feedbacks are also obtained from students. Students acknowledged the relevance and challenges of working on real-world projects, particularly in a foreign country that they were unfamiliar with. The opportunity to work with managers from a different country and to apply the theories learnt into practical applications is another important appealing factor of the project collaboration. While the COVID-19 pandemic resulted in the cancellation of the Indonesia trip, students still appreciated the chance to understand the banking industry in Indonesia.

The following are four selected students' feedback:

Feedback #1: This study mission gave me the opportunity to immerse myself in a completely different culture. If not for the study mission, I wouldn't have visited Laos and learnt about the people and culture there. Most importantly, I have learnt to be adaptable, especially in situations where I am working with different people or when I am in a different country.

Feedback #2: When working with Company A, we often did not have sufficient information or data that are of sufficient quality, and we had to work around that. Furthermore, we had to figure out the direction of our project and our final product by ourselves, so I appreciate the independence we were given to challenge ourselves.

Feedback #3: In my opinion, this course enables me to not only understand the traditions, culture and working ethics of another country, like Indonesia, but also be exposed to business and accounting concepts which are necessary in analysing the current business products, market and financial capabilities. Additionally, this course also challenged me to bridge the knowledge of what I have to what is required. Furthermore, through this course, I have learnt how to structure and format a persuasive recommendation.

Feedback #4: Despite not being able to go to Indonesia, I have learnt new information about Indonesia from other students and the professor, as well as the sharing by Indonesian experts. Being able to work with Bank B helped increase my understanding of Indonesian banking landscape and gave me a more open-minded view of how business differs across different countries.

Partnership Management and Benefits of Project Collaboration with University

Partnership management is a key component to the success of PBL. Both SMU and the project sponsors (Company A and Bank B) had taken care to manage the partnership in four key aspects.

First, the value proposition of the study mission was clearly established. By participating in the study mission, both students and university faculties were able to learn about the Laotian and Indonesian economy and business environment. Students also enhanced their learning by working on real-world projects. At the same time, the project sponsors were able to benefit from the ideas and recommendations provided by the students through the projects.

Second, both SMU and the project sponsors were committed to deep collaborations on the projects. Students and faculty from SMU spent a total of 14 weeks working on the projects in close collaboration with five senior executives from Company A as well as four senior managers from

Bank B. When students made their final presentations to Company A, the full senior management team, including the company's president, was on hand to listen and provide feedback to the students. Likewise, during the final presentation session to Bank B, all the four senior managers as well as the Head of New Digital Ventures of Bank B dialled in and listened to all the four online presentations held over WebEx.

Third, there was extensive knowledge creation and exchange between SMU and the industry partners. As part of the projects, students created solutions including balanced scorecards, business dashboards, and valuation models that were readily adopted and implemented by Company A. Similarly, recommendations on how to penetrate the education industry and increase usage rate of online banking application of Bank B were feasible and can be pursued by Bank B. Students and faculty also benefited from the knowledge gained from the unique opportunity to work with senior executives of one of the most prominent family businesses in Laos as well as a regional bank based in Jakarta.

Fourth, the partnership was greatly enhanced by the continuous feedback offered by all parties. Early in the collaboration, the regular feedback and communication between university faculties, Company A, and Bank B were crucial in developing projects that were realistic, relevant, and beneficial to both students and the company. Throughout the collaboration, both Company A and Bank B also offered clear feedback on their expectations of the projects. This provided clear guidance to both the faculty and students on key project deliverables.

Conclusions

By drawing upon two case studies of a university–industry overseas consulting programme, we summarise and highlight students' major takeaways from the course, and the essentials of partnership management. For any partnership to work, understanding each other's role is important. In particular, the case studies have shown that university pedagogy may have to evolve with times to satisfy the requirements of employers in the present and the future. It is clear that university education plays an important role in equipping and nurturing digital literacy and cultural intelligence within students.

Part 1 of this chapter was first published in the 23 April 2019 issue of Business Times under the title "Enhancing SMEs' Data Analytics Capability Through University Tie-Ups".

Part 2 of this chapter was first published in the 13 May 2020 issue of Business Times under the title "Developing Online Business Strategy with Millennials through Partnership with University."

Part 3 of this chapter was adapted from 2021 Volume 9 (2) issue of International Journal of Education, pages 1 to 12 under the title "Enhancing Cultural Intelligence and Digital Literacy in Accounting Education: Insights from a University's Global Student Consulting Programme."

4

SMEs Roadmap to Navigate through the Artificial Intelligence and Data Analytics Revolution

Background

As big corporations rush to jump on the bandwagon with significant investments into new technology, small and medium-sized enterprises (SMEs) are sometimes faced with the overwhelming challenge of not having the capabilities to catch on and are at risk of being left behind. At the same time, adopters of Artificial Intelligence and Data Analytics (AIDA) often overemphasise the technology aspect while neglecting the results and findings which can be acted upon, leading to failed investments. This chapter seeks to provide a roadmap to help SMEs navigate through the AIDA revolution in a way that will allow them to kickstart their own digital transformation journey. This will ensure that they adopt the right AIDA tools that provide appropriate solutions to business problems they are looking to solve.

The Rise of Artificial Intelligence and Data Analytics

Artificial Intelligence (AI) is all around us: in our mobile phones, watches, cars, home appliances, in our dining and retail experiences, in our offices, in public services, throughout media and beyond. Having weathered through waves of winters over the decades, AI in its latest form promises to fundamentally change our everyday living and seemingly *abracadabra* away our problems with the wave of the AI magic wand. The growing hype surrounding AI's advancement in recent years has led to several observers making damning claims about how AI will soon take over multitudes of jobs, rendering a big percentage of the current workforce jobless. That may be somewhat of an overstatement because at present, the part of human intelligence that AI is capable of replicating is only in prediction. Prediction is a critical component of AI and is the reason why AI is so powerful today.

Along with AI, Data Analytics (DA) has also been front and centre of the digital disruption driven by Industry 4.0. As a process, DA involves evaluating data to address business questions by using technology to transform vast amounts of available data into knowledge and insight. Together, AIDA is spearheading a revolution that is radically changing society, regulators, and the world.

Understanding AI

Before adopting AIDA into daily business operations, it is necessary to cut through the current AI hype by bringing across a clear definition of what AI is and how it will partner with human intelligence in revolutionising businesses and industries. This needs to start from being able to clearly distinguish between what is tangible and possible versus what is straight out of a sci-fi novel/film/television show.

Russell and Norvig (2021) use AI as a term describing machines which mimic human cognitive functions like "learning" and "problem-solving". Where the word "AI" is used, the term "machine learning (ML)" is likely to be found close-by too. ML, a subfield of AI and the engine that drives most of AI's recent progress, is defined as "the study of computer algorithms that improve automatically through experience" (Mitchell, 1997). In essence, AI and ML (in their current forms) consist of techniques which learn to recognise patterns in order to make predictions that facilitate decision-making.

Going deeper with AI and ML has also brought forth more sophisticated techniques like Natural Language Processing (NLP) which combines learning with linguistics, allowing for intelligent analysis of written languages. Advanced AI and ML systems have also allowed machines to produce more accurate results than humans, particularly for areas which involve repetitive work. The ever-increasing hype of AI is therefore not without legitimacy. AI systems are promising and powerful decision tools for organisations across different industries to adopt. The next preparatory step in looking into how AIDA can be implemented is to identify the fundamental trends that allow for these tools to be feasibly adopted.

Trend Enablers of AIDA

For AIDA to gain a strong foothold in today's world, it leans heavily on four trend enablers: **ABCD**.

Availability of affordable and powerful machines: Rapid technological advancement has opened the doors for the exponential growth of computing power. This has been accompanied by tumbling costs of computing. While some technology observers claimed that Moore's Law would reach its limits by 2020, the phenomenon whereby higher computing power follows lowering computing costs is very much alive despite the negative impacts COVID-19 has had on consumer electronics.

Back when the hype of AI manifested mainly in science fiction films and tv shows, the cost of large-scale implementation made it infeasible and impracticable. The IBM 3380, in 1980, was the first hard disk drive to have a storage capacity of 1 gigabyte (GB) and had to be housed in a cabinet, making the 250 kg device almost as big as a refrigerator. Contrast that with the first commercially available 1-terabyte (TB) SD card (just slightly bigger than a $1 coin) released by Lexar in January 2019, and it is obvious how readily available storage space is. The Lexar 1TB cost US$500 in 2019, high by today's standards, that is less than 0.5% of the IBM 3380 which cost upward of US$100,000. Moore's Law continues to hold true three years on (in 2022), as Amazon listings price the Lexar 1TB under US$200.

Enhanced computing power also comes in the form of drastically improved processing speed. Technology experts have noted what might have taken weeks to process a decade ago can now be done in minutes. Affordability, portability, and speed are the reasons why AI has now become readily available to businesses for implementation, adoption, and use.

Better algorithms for use: Much like computing power, AI techniques and algorithms have also seen great improvement in recent times. With a multitude of research poured into evolving and advancing the fundamental algorithms behind AI, there is now a whole suite of AI techniques which can be used to solve a variety of different problems. A growing community of developers continuously revise and refine these algorithms while also consolidating them into packages that are accessible for free through open-source programming languages like R and Python.

In the past, programming and coding were seen as extremely technical and even agonising to do. But today, R and Python's plethora of libraries and packages of AI and ML, coupled with developer communities such as GitHub and Stack Overflow (among many others) have opened the gates for businesses to pick and choose AI algorithms suited for their work.

Cloud computing: This has given AIDA a platform to shine by providing improved accessibility that goes beyond hardware and device storage. Companies have begun migrating to cloud-based platforms so as to run operations directly from the cloud without being bogged down by physical limitations. Cloud providers like Google Cloud integrate AI and ML services into application programming interfaces (API) that allow for businesses to develop customised DA solutions to their problems for themselves and their clients. Cloud platforms also make data storage, computing power and graphic processing units (GPU) scalable, thereby enabling algorithms to work more efficiently without the restrictions of on-site hardware. Deep learning using Neural Networks has proven to work at least 10 times faster with cloud-based GPU acceleration as compared to the regular computer processing units (CPUs).

Data are everywhere: Traditionally, data collected for analysis have primarily been numerical and structured. The boom and influx of Big Data, supplemented by the growing number of social media platforms, has led to an unprecedented "hunger" for data of all sorts, including images, text, and videos. These kinds of data are unstructured and were previously not thought of as usable for AIDA. However, Big Data storage systems, whether physical or cloud-based, have now allowed for the storage of unstructured data as well as the processing of these data. A good example is Apache Hadoop, a powerful analytics engine for Big Data.

These ABCD trend enablers put AIDA in a prime position to revolutionise how businesses operate and how people work in the years to come, making them a valuable resource for SMEs to tap on.

Getting Started with AIDA

Some SMEs have already started their AIDA journey by using ML techniques to shape their business processes and decision-making with the ultimate aim of raising profitability through revenue improvement, cost reduction and new sources of value creation.

ML is seen as a continuation of the concepts around predictive analytics. However, a key difference in ML is that it uses mathematical algorithms to train computers in the processing and analysing of large amounts of data, allowing them to produce rules, identify patterns and generate classification predictions.

The first step is for SMEs to identify what data to use and analyse. For instance, if an SME intends to predict customer behaviour, relevant data to gather may include the following:

(1) **Customer Data**: These relate to customer profile and purchase patterns.
(2) **Social Media Data**: These include the wealth of knowledge about customers, their preferences, opinions, and locations that can be harvested from social media.
(3) **Web Traffic Data**: If the SME has a website, then the company should ideally have useful data about who has visited and what customers did on the site. This information may be useful for understanding clients and developing a corresponding sales strategy.

Essentially, data is the core of any ML algorithm and the foundation of AIDA. It must be supplied in the form that algorithms understand. The main function of algorithms is to then unlock the concealed information and knowledge available in the data.

Here are two examples of ML-enabled tasks used by some SMEs:

- **Spend Analytics**: With the help of improved data storage capabilities, there is now greater ease for SMEs to collect and gather data involving anything on which they spend money. Such data include purchase orders, billed invoices, card transactions, employee claims relating to travel, medical and flexible benefits.

  Based on the mathematical distances between points, **clustering** methods iteratively compare voluminous transactions with each other and form clusters which have similar properties. Since this is a purely mathematical process, bias can be reduced significantly. This allows new insights to be gathered from the data, which was previously unknown or not quantified.

  This should ultimately provide answers to questions such as "Who is buying?", "Who is selling?", "What is being bought?", "How many?", "When is the transaction?" and "What is the mode of payment?" among others — all of which are the very questions that revolve around the work that procurement does to add value to companies.

  Exploring clustering and its variants are but the first foray into spend analytics for SMEs looking to better manage spending. Through the use of text analytics combined with NLP, text information can be converted into data for a more advanced analysis of expenditure data. In risk management, text analytics can help classify transactions into "high risk", "medium risk" and "low risk" using classification methods such as decision trees, k-nearest neighbours, and neural networks to analyse historical records. Using the analysis findings, these algorithms can predict whether a transaction is likely to be "high risk" and procurement can step in to block such a payment before any money is lost.

- **Sales Demand Prediction**: With previous years of sales data, SMEs are able to identify patterns in sales and consumption. This can be done on an individual basis or focus on a target group or demographic. Probability algorithms are the key to envisioning certainty into the future. The base of probability, which is the likelihood of an event occurring, can either be 0 or 1, which is to say impossible or certain. The algorithms take into account all external and internal influential factors that go into the sales process and the likelihood of that process being a success.

This type of "what if" analysis allows sales managers to understand the impact of these factors on sales numbers and evaluate how to use these insights as levers so as to have a greater positive impact on sales. In addition, ML is able to optimise marketing spends and processes, as well as increase the sales per amount spent on advertisements and product promotion in the market.

The solution can be as simple as a **regression analysis** based on year-on-year comparisons where the process simulates different marketing scenarios and results so as to identify the optimal marketing strategy in real-life conditions. The underlying concept behind regression analysis is that an output is explained by a combination of multiple variables.

In the above example, each marketing scenario, along with other influencing factors are the multiple variables used to predict the output of "sales per amount spent", using a regression model. The optimal regression model is one which, when compared to others, has the smallest error. While these algorithms are not without error, the continuous improvement of them coupled with more accurate and relevant data being used for analysis will help improve accuracy and can potentially provide SMEs with quantifiable sales demand figures, allowing for managers to make better decisions for their business.

Besides recognising AIDA's potential from a technology angle, it is also crucial to consider the impact that AIDA can have on SMEs from a business perspective.

Impact on SMEs

As Industry 4.0 extends its reach into many aspects of everyday life, AIDA has been afforded the fertile ground that it previously lacked to now thrive. AIDA has drastically altered the business environment while concurrently enabling businesses to adapt to these changes by transforming their processes and products while constantly innovating and improving their operations. As such, the ball is now in SMEs' court, and it is up to them to make the next move.

In response to changing market conditions, AIDA tools affording predictive analytics capabilities can help with improving forecast accuracy. By tapping on real-time internal and external data, thereby allowing SMEs to lower their exposure to risk, SMEs can then better manage their assets and resources with a view to seeking out new innovation opportunities. Within the SMEs, which are often plagued by administrative bottlenecks as they do not have enough manpower, automation facilitated by AIDA tools can help overcome this limitation and further improve their overall efficiency and business routines.

In their 2021 South East Asia (SEA) Social Commerce Report, iKala, a Taiwanese start-up offering AI-based customer acquisition and engagement platform services to clients, identified social commerce as a growing business trend in SEA. Their report combined with findings and data from Hootsuite, We Are Social, McKinsey, and Facebook identified several internal benefits that AIDA can bring to SMEs if well implemented into the business:

- **Saving Time and Money**: AIDA integrated with automation systems allows for tasks to be completed faster than before with manual processes now either simplified or automated. For example, marketing campaigns can be monitored and tracked using scripts that can be written to flag out matters that call for human intervention. Instead of constant supervision, staff are only required to take action when something out of the ordinary happens. Time can be better spent on higher-order activities that cannot be replicated by scripts and algorithms, bringing both time savings and cost savings.
- **Increased Productivity**: With time savings allowing staff to switch their attention away from routine tasks, AIDA opens the door to higher operational efficiencies. For example, scripts and algorithms trained through text analytics can streamline customer interaction by directing simple queries to chatbots. This frees up much-needed resources to be redeployed to urgent matters that require a more personable approach and improves customer engagement. Through the optimisation of business routines, product quality can be improved, resource consumption reduced, and throughput increased. Similarly, analysis findings from implementing AIDA can facilitate optimal decision-making because staff can use AIDA tools to overcome their struggle with raw data and mind-boggling statistics.

- **Increased Revenue/Profitability**: As a direct effect of improved productivity, overall sales/profitability is given a significant uplift too because AIDA tools enable more precise tracking and recording. For instance, sales representatives can use a platform combining AIDA tracking tools with the analysis of words to help them identify the effectiveness of their sales practices. A further integration with customer relationship management (CRM) platforms can bridge the gap between sales and marketing teams by offering approaches tailored to customers to win new ones and retain current ones.

- **Improved Strategic Management**: AIDA provides SME's management with greater oversight of operations, client needs, market fluctuations, and staff performance. With timelier data-driven analysis findings, management can gain a better oversight of their companies' internal operations, a better understanding of the needs of clients and partners, as well as a broader perspective of local, regional, and global markets. From these data, they will be able to develop, modify, and adapt their corporate strategies that could involve enhancing R&D, developing new products and services, optimising production and delivery, and targeted marketing to customers. This should come together with the second mindset shift discussed in Chapter 1.

- **Level Playing Field with Big Corporations**: While big corporations tend to have big budgets to tap into when embarking on their digitalisation journey, SMEs often do not have that luxury. What they lack in financial resources, they can make up for in being small and agile enough to quickly pivot and respond to dynamic changes in business environments. Doing so requires an agile and experimentation mindset, previously mentioned in Chapter 1 as the third mindset shift, and often begins with senior stakeholders and decision makers. With them on board in spearheading technology change, SMEs can take gradual small steps in adopting AIDA into their workflows and unlock their "small player advantage".

As with all things, with benefits, there always comes costs. Furthermore, such benefits are never guaranteed given certain limitations. Some of these costs and limitations are discussed in the following and are coupled with suggestions on how to overcome them:

- **Technical Difficulties**: These include data and systems issues. While the ideal is for AIDA tools to provide cost and time savings, SMEs may quickly find out that the automation and streamlining of their operations and processes are not as easy as first thought, given that there are some tasks that require the human element, especially those that are subjective in nature. As a result, instead of saving time, staff are now burdened with twice the amount of work having to deal with learning new tools and still intervening manually. SMEs may also face the "lack of usable data" problem as they may not have systems to collect, consolidate, and store data previously.

  However, this should not deter SMEs from taking the first steps into exploring AIDA. With proper training, staff can learn to distinguish between tasks that can be automated and those that require manual intervention. They can then use AIDA tools to automate a portion of the operations before stepping in when they are required to. Furthermore, the nature of the ML algorithms behind the AIDA tools means that the automation process improves with time if trained well.

  To overcome the lack of data, SMEs can begin by building their data pipeline with external data sources while improving their existing available data. This would ensure that they have sufficient volume of data to carry out analysis when they first venture into using AIDA tools. As they gradually build up an internal data source that is comprehensive and large enough, they can then retrain their models and make necessary adjustments.[1]

- **Lack of Buy-In**: To be able to unlock the benefits of increased productivity and revenue/profits, there needs to be buy-in from employees and management, which more often than not is the greatest stumbling block. The lack of buy-in tends to stem from a psychological resistance to change, a long-standing phenomenon, particularly in relation to technological innovation. Schmidt *et al.* (2020) found that accounting professionals cling to the status quo of using the tools that

---

[1] Amount of data varies from company to company. For some, data in the thousands is already considered large enough while for others, even millions of data points is considered small. Typically, linear models can perform well with just a few hundred data points while non-linear ones such as classification trees and neural networks will need at least a few thousand to achieve decent model performance.

they are familiar with instead of emergent DA tools partially due to the bureaucracy and hierarchy in their firms as well as the high pressure of getting the job done under time constraints. This is not unique to accountants *per se*, with many other sectors such as education, healthcare, human resource also hindered by this.

Overcoming this resistance and fear among staff starts with educating them on the potential efficiencies of AIDA adoption as well as affording them time to accommodate these tools into their daily work gradually. This can help make them more receptive to trying these new tools out without the worry of their work being disrupted. As they grow to be more engaged with the use of AIDA tools, they can begin to see the value that the tools bring to their overall performance at work.

Should the lack of buy-in stem from not having the necessary technical skills to utilise these AIDA tools, tapping into grants, subsidies, and incentives that governments make available to SMEs for digital transformation can help train and equip staff appropriately. These support schemes have been accelerated in part due to the impact of COVID-19 and can alleviate the financial pressures that SMEs face in adopting new technology.

- **Strategic Misalignment**: Due to the hype of AIDA, many business leaders have had their fair share of brushes with it. The potential of AIDA can sometimes drive them into making misguided investments into technology without fully understanding the practical aspects of adoption and how that would impact business operations. This creates a strategic misalignment where management desires AIDA to be implemented as part of the company's digitalisation journey, but operationally, there is no clear direction on how AIDA can actually improve operations. As Krunic (2020) suggests, this has led to many failed investments into technology where time and money spent do not amount to desired outcomes.

As clichéd as this may sound, this can be solved when management decides on a clear strategic direction that they should take with regard to their pathway to adopting AIDA. Since adoption is a process, management needs to devise a plan and have the right talents in place to chart the SME's course. Rather than implementing AIDA wholesale into every aspect of the SME's operations, it may be wise to start from the simple tasks first before building up. When the SME is aligned strategically from top to bottom, everyone becomes encouraged that their adoption of AIDA today is done with the long-term future in mind.

Example: NaRaYa

iKala's report highlighted NaRaYa, a Thai handbag brand, which experimented with social commerce in 2020 combining iKala's Shoplus Order Management System with KOL Radar's AI influencer marketing platform, and in doing so, streamlined its order management process. This brought a 50% increase in purchases, a 90% increase in order management efficiency, and an overall increase in customer interaction. A bolstered social media presence helped reinforce customer loyalty and opened doors to a new customer segment of social commerce.

NaRaYa is but one of many SMEs that have taken the plunge in the deep end by intentionally seeking out AIDA-related services in recent times, especially in light of a global pandemic. However, a collaborative study done between November 2018 and April 2020 by Singapore Institute of Technology (SIT), RSM Singapore, and the Institute of Singapore Chartered Accountants (ISCA) found that nearly 70% of Singapore SMEs have yet to adopt DA. Among them, about half had no intention to do so in the future either, citing data protection and privacy concerns as well as scepticism towards whether DA would actually benefit them. Perhaps a further year in the pandemic wilderness might have since changed their stance on AIDA adoption, but what cannot be missed is that this technology cynicism needs to be overcome before SMEs will be willing to hop onto the bandwagon.

Encouraging AIDA Adoption

Some of the scepticism may have originated from the false starts that led to several AI winters in the past decades. Prior to the pandemic in 2019, Gartner identified three top challenges to AI/ML adoption: (1) skills, (2) fear of the unknown, and (3) data scope or quality. In line with the

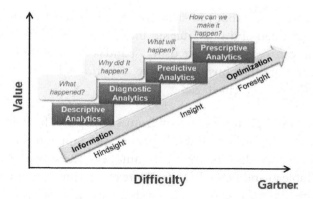

Figure 1.   Gartner's Stages of Analytics Model

previously discussed suggestions on overcoming technical difficulties, these three barriers are not as insurmountable as SMEs may imagine initially.

What is thought of as going into the unknown may come from a lack of awareness and misunderstanding of the true nature of AIDA. Instead of fearing the unknown, SMEs can take their important first steps into basic analytics and build up their data maturity before advancing to AIDA.

One of the simple models that can be used is Gartner's Stages of Analytics which breaks down the analytics process into four stages: Descriptive, Diagnostic, Predictive and Prescriptive (see Figure 1).

Descriptive: It aims to describe "what happened" through the examination of historical data for the purpose of making informed decisions and forms the majority of analytics work. Techniques associated with descriptive analytics categorise, characterise, consolidate, and classify data to convert it into useful information that supports the understanding and analysis of business performance. The output of descriptive analytics tends to come in the form of charts and reports that summarise data. This would involve the use of visualisations and dashboards for exploratory data analysis (EDA) as well as for the purpose of presenting the useful information and insights drawn. EDA can be carried out using dashboarding tools like Tableau and Microsoft PowerBI or using plotting tools in visualisation packages such as "matplotlib" (for Python) and "ggplot2" (for R). Before EDA can be done,

SMEs need to ensure that raw data are retrieved and then transformed, formatted, encoded and manipulated into formats that are readable and usable. This can be carried out using "pandas" (for Python) or "dplyr" (for R). Carrying out robust descriptive analytics will allow for a deeper analysis in the subsequent stages.

Diagnostic: It is typically a build-on from Descriptive, further examining the data to answer the "why did it happen?" question and is characterised by drill-down and data discovery techniques. These are often already built-into Tableau and PowerBI to facilitate answering "why". The answers, however, are not provided by the techniques or tools themselves but requires users to interpret the outputs from the analysis and visualisations.

For SMEs, drill-down techniques applied to their datasets should be building on the findings from the earlier analysis and should also flag out anomalies that call for further investigation. As diagnostic analysis tends to be qualitative and non-technical, it is important that the analysts involved in this already have acquired a significant domain understanding of the business. Ideally, these should be seasoned employees who have picked up skills in AIDA.

Predictive: It often uses results from Descriptive and Diagnostic to find answers for "what will happen?", using historical data to make future predictions based on a current set of variables. This is where AI starts to come in, with ML techniques being used to determine the impact of those variables on the predicted output which can be an extrapolation of historical data into the future. However, Predictive does not necessarily have to be preceded by Diagnostic. In other words, Predictive can be done after Descriptive while skipping over Diagnostic.

Prescriptive: It draws on the inputs from Predictive to enable better decisions about what needs to be done, in doing so, answers the "how can we make it happen?". The primary focus of Prescriptive is to find the best course of action which in essence should facilitate the decision-making process. Prescriptive models tend to revolve around the "optimal", combining probability, statistics with constraints, uncertainty, and decision alternatives. Applying ML techniques to Prescriptive will therefore identify and extract rules that relate to the predicted output.

Adopting Gartner's Stages of Analytics model already requires some level of technical understanding of analytics and the above details on each stage can be implemented at a more rudimentary level for SMEs which are embarking on their first foray into AIDA. Another way to implement the model can be just to start with Descriptive Analytics only, using the more familiar Microsoft Excel functionalities. Having this model as a reference can provide SMEs a more comfortable first stepping stone and they can be encouraged to dive further into AIDA.

Conclusions

In September 2021, *Harvard Business Review* (HBR) published an article discussing the rise in AI adoption as a result of the COVID crisis. Over the 18-month period after the pandemic began its siege around the world, AIDA experienced an accelerated adoption as businesses began asking questions about using their data effectively. Businesses have begun to see the instrumental role that AI plays in improving productivity, making up for the labour skills shortage, offering new products and services, and tackling supply chain problems. As such, SMEs can no longer dismiss AIDA technology as a good-to-have or risk being outdone by big corporates and competitors willing to take the plunge into AIDA adoption.

While ML is a powerful AIDA tool, SMEs need to be cautioned that it is not the solution to every problem. Sometimes, a simple solution that uses basic analytics as mentioned in the previous section is already enough. There are also many instances where certain ML algorithms or pre-processing methods actually give poorer performance measure numbers and as such, suggesting that ML may not be applicable.

References

Gartner (2019). 3 Barriers to AI Adoption. *Smarter with Gartner*. https://www.gartner.com/smarterwithgartner/3-barriers-to-ai-adoption.

Mitchell, T. (1997). *Machine Learning*. New York, US: McGraw Hill.

Russell, S. and Norvig, P. (2021). *Artificial Intelligence: A Modern Approach (AIMA) Global Edition*. Harlow, UK: Pearson Education Limited.

5

How Accounting Organisations Can Approach Digital Transformation

Background

In recent years, accounting organisations have embarked on various digital transformation efforts as they seek to benefit from technological advancements. This chapter discusses how accounting organisations can approach digital transformation from three key aspects. First, it examines how data analytics is reshaping the work of accountants. Second, it explores how technological advances have led to the emergence of continuous auditing and how it can play a role in finance and audit. Finally, this chapter illustrates how technology is allowing accounting organisations to develop robust methods of detecting fraudulent activity.

Part 1: How Data Analytics is Reshaping the Work of Accountants

According to the 2016 State of Analytics and Data Science report published by data analytics firm Mu Sigma, 65% of senior business leaders surveyed in the United States (US) believe that data analytics has influenced their business in a positive way.

As businesses increasingly try to position themselves to reap benefits from data analytics, accountants are poised to play a leading role in managing that transition. Indeed, the same survey by Mu Sigma found that Chief Financial Officers (CFOs) were the second largest group of executives who had overall responsibility for analytics at their workplaces (after Chief Information Officers (CIOs)).

Certainly, accountants are at a distinct advantage when implementing data analytics because they not only have ready access to financial data but also often have a keen understanding of how that data can help their companies retain a strategic advantage over competitors in the modern business environment.

Johann Xavier, the Regional CFO for Asia Pacific and Greater China for Saatchi & Saatchi, expressed a similar sentiment in a recent interview when he commented that the "new generation of CFOs should take advantage of their ability to derive more robust and revealing conclusions from the analysis of financial data."

Applications of data analytics in accounting

Data analytics can certainly play a key role in many aspects of accounting. Here are some ways that data analytics can enhance the work that accountants do and the contributions that they make to the wider organisation:

- **Boost competitiveness**: Predictive analytics techniques can boost a company's competitiveness and profitability by allowing accounting professionals to make more accurate and detailed forecasts. Such forecasts enable the company to anticipate and react more quickly to market trends that would otherwise be difficult to foresee.
- **Enhance financial reporting**: As companies increasingly move towards the adoption of Integrated Reporting — which seeks to create a "concise communication about how an organisation's strategy, governance, performance and prospects, in the context of its external environment, lead to the creation of value in the short, medium and long term" — more sophisticated data analytics tools can allow companies to link diverse financial and non-financial datasets to provide more comprehensive and rigorous reporting of their performance to shareholders and other stakeholders.
- **Manage risks**: Over time, the role of the accounting and finance function in managing risks has evolved from being one that is primarily

focused on compliance and internal controls to one where it is also equally likely to involve assessing risks arising from a diverse range of other areas, such as the regulatory environment, the supply chain, or even from business strategy. Data analytics techniques, such as continuous auditing and continuous monitoring, can help accounting and finance professionals to assess and manage relevant risk levels within their organisations.

- **Identify fraud**: Data analytics techniques are well suited to detecting fraud. Emerging technologies in this area can allow a forensic accountant to quickly and effectively sieve through large volumes of transactions to identify anomalies in data which can often be indicative of fraudulent activity.

While data analytics presents a range of opportunities for accountants and their organisations, many still find themselves at the beginning of their journeys and have some way to go before they can extend their capabilities to fully reap the potential benefits.

Highlighting this, the Chartered Global Management Accountants recently surveyed C-level executives from 16 countries and found that almost a third of respondents feel that big data has made things worse, not better, for decision making in their organisations.

Growing data analytics capabilities

To develop strong capabilities in data analytics that suit their needs, accountants, together with the rest of their organisations, should first work to develop a clear plan that articulates how three key component parts, i.e., data, analytics, and people, can be strategically integrated and aligned to create business values.

In particular, building a strong data foundation is key to the success of any data analytics strategy. In addition to identifying external and internal data sets that will be needed for analysis, planners also need to ensure that relevant data is treated and managed in such a way that allows it to be used across a range of analytics applications.

Achieving this often involves making considerable investments in new data capabilities, and may also require substantial reorganisation of existing data architectures.

A good data analytics strategy should also address the potential trade-offs that a company must inevitably make between the time or cost that it takes to implement data analytics and the potential business value that can be generated from it.

Another critical but often neglected component of a successful data analytics programme is the people who are tasked to run it. In order to maximise the value it extracts from data analytics, an organisation must ensure that it leverages talent with the appropriate skillsets and abilities.

Accountants must develop relevant skillsets in order to ensure that they continue to play a key role in driving data analytics initiatives within their organisations. This was recognised in a recent study of Singapore-based CFOs undertaken by accounting firm Ernst & Young and CPA Australia. In anticipation of the accounting and finance function taking on greater responsibility for data analytics, the report identified "analysis and advisory skills" as one of the key skills that a forward-looking CFO needs in his tool kit. It further noted that "CFOs of the future will need analytical skills to enable them to find the areas where efficiencies can be gained."

However, one key obstacle to raising data analytics capabilities in the accounting function is the global shortage of talent in this area. A recent study by the Association of Accountants and Finance Professionals in Business and the recruitment firm Robert Half made clear that companies in North America face a huge challenge in hiring accounting and finance professionals who also possess requisite skills in both data analytics and accounting and finance. In Singapore, the situation is no different, with the 2016 Harvey Nash/KPMG CIO survey recently identifying data analytics to be the most in-demand skill in Singapore for the second year running.

One way for CFOs to overcome the talent shortage is for hiring managers to look to assemble teams that, as a whole, possess all the requisite skillsets rather than try to look for all those skillsets in a single individual. The creation of such multidisciplinary teams would allow a group of individuals, each possessing specialised skills in data analytics, accounting and finance, or other technical areas, to work together to effectively execute the broader data analytics strategy.

Conclusion

Overall, there is a need for a greater push from accountants to embrace data analytics in all aspects of their work. Whether in applying data analytics to provide more value in their current scope of work or in working with multidimensional teams to execute broader data analytics strategies, the accountant must expect to play a leading role as companies continue with their relentless drive to incorporate data analytics into the way they run their businesses.

Part 2: Introducing Continuous Auditing in Finance and Audit

In the past decade, rapid technological developments have led to the widespread adoption of enterprise resource planning systems. These ERP platforms not only allow different functional areas of a business to share data but also enable businesses to generate financial information in real time. Such developments have fundamentally altered how businesses operate and present both challenges and opportunities for CFOs and auditors.

That's because traditional audit methods have, to a significant extent, not kept up with these developments. Many audit procedures that are used today remain manual in nature and are often costly in terms of both time and money. To a large degree, it is as a result of these associated costs that audits are only conducted on an annual basis today.

One emerging automation concept/technology that is gaining prominence in audit is the continuous audit. A cost-effective method of incorporating a continuous audit might be to develop a continuous audit system that is programmed to trigger an audit after a certain number of accounts-receivable transactions have been made in the ERP system.

Seven dimensions of continuous audit

According to the American Institute of Certified Public Accountants and the Canadian Institute of Chartered Accountants, the continuous audit is "a methodology that enables independent auditors to provide written assurance on a subject matter, for which an entity's management is responsible, using a series of auditors' reports issued virtually simultaneously with, or a short period of time after, the occurrence of events underlying the subject matter."

While the idea of the continuous audit is not new, it was introduced almost 20 years ago, and key conceptual elements of continuous auditing have largely remained intact since then — auditors have, up till now, faced many challenges in implementing it. However, with rapid advancements in information technology, the growth of big data, and the increasing adoption of data analytics in business in recent years, the widespread implementation of continuous auditing by both internal and external auditors is within the reach of many companies today.

Building on traditional practices in auditing, continuous auditing introduces innovation along seven key dimensions to enable real-time assurance and enhancement of the reliability of real-time financial information.

Dimension 1: Continuous Real-Time Audits

Real-time audits that occur continuously represent the goal of continuous audits. For example, a cost-effective method of incorporating a continuous audit might be to develop a continuous audit system that is programmed to trigger an audit after a certain number of accounts-receivable transactions have been made in the ERP system.

Dimension 2: Proactive Audit Models

Audits have traditionally been conducted on an annual basis. When audits are only conducted once a year, material errors, omissions, or fraud can often go undetected for long periods before they are flagged by an audit. Conversely, continuous audits are conducted on a continuous basis. This would allow auditors to proactively detect and look into exceptions as they occur rather than react to them long after they have occurred — as is frequently the case with traditional audits.

Dimension 3: Automation

Traditional audits rely heavily on manual procedures and are thus often time- and labour-intensive. The automation of audit procedures in a continuous audit can substantially reduce these constraints. In order to increase the effectiveness of the automation process, it is important to ensure the standardisation of data collection and the formalisation of internal control policies.

The standardisation of data collection would increase the gains that can be made from automation by reducing the time spent by the auditor on manually cleaning data before the performance of automated audit procedures. Furthermore, the formalisation of internal control policies would provide well-defined procedures that the automated procedures could follow to ensure that they can run smoothly, without any human intervention.

A continuous audit would consider the entire population of transactions in both monitoring and testing. This would enhance the effectiveness of the audit and raise the probability of detecting material errors, omissions, fraud, and internal control violations.

Dimension 4: Evolution of the Work of Auditors
In a continuous audit environment, much of the audit task will be automated. Hence, the bulk of the auditor's work will be focused on more complex activities, such as those dealing with estimates and judgement verification, where he or she would need to display judgment and professional scepticism.

To a large extent, the main role of the auditor in a continuous audit environment would involve investigating and resolving exceptions generated by the continuous auditing system.

Dimension 5: Nature, Timing, and Extent of Auditing
The continuous auditing methodology substantially alters the nature of traditional audit testing. In traditional audits, manual internal control and substantive detailed testing are performed periodically to evaluate managers' assertions. In contrast, continuous auditing can be divided into two distinct but complimentary aspects: continuous controls monitoring (CCM) and continuous data assurance (CDA).

CCM refers to the process where the continuous auditing system continuously monitors internal controls for violations, while CDA refers to the process where transactional data are continuously tested for anomalies.

The timing of the performance of various audit tasks is different in a continuous audit. In traditional audits, internal control testing typically takes place in the planning stage of the audit, while substantive detail testing takes place in the fieldwork stage. In contrast, both internal controls monitoring and transaction data testing should occur at the same time in a continuous audit.

The scope of the continuous audit is also more extensive than traditional audits. The labour- and time-intensive nature of traditional audits makes it impractical to include the whole population of transactions in testing. Instead, a representative sample of the whole population is often used.

In comparison, a continuous audit would consider the entire population of transactions in both monitoring and testing. This would enhance the effectiveness of the audit and raise the probability of detecting material errors, omissions, fraud, and internal control violations within the continuous audit environment.

Dimension 6: Data Modelling and Data Analytics

Analytical procedures in traditional audits typically employ basic statistical techniques, such as ratio and trend analyses. In comparison, more sophisticated data modelling and analytics techniques are used in the continuous audit. In particular, data modelling and data analytics are applied to transaction data and account balances for monitoring and testing in the continuous auditing environment.

Dimension 7: Nature and Timing of Audit Reports

In traditional audits, audit reports are issued, after every audit, on an annual basis. In the continuous auditing environment, information generated by an ERP system is assumed to be free of material errors, omissions, or fraud unless an audit exception report indicates otherwise.

Conclusions

Undeniably, organisations have become more complex today. They have elaborate and integrated business processes, and often also have to deal with ever-increasing legislation and regulations. Like all other aspects of business, the audit function must evolve to keep up with these complexities. While continuous audit remains very much an emerging field, broad forces that will shape its evolution and nature are rapidly coming into focus. Consequently, the demand for the continuous audit will certainly continue to grow in the coming years.

Part 3: How Forensic Accounting Can Move Forward with Technology

In June 2009, Bernie Madoff, a former chairman of the NASDAQ stock exchange, was sentenced to 150 years in prison for operating the largest Ponzi scheme in US history. Over the course of several decades, Madoff had systematically defrauded investors of up to US$65 billion, engaging in illegal activities including securities fraud, money laundering, and making false filings with the US Securities and Exchange Commission (SEC).

While the scale of the US$65 billion scam was eye-catching, what was perhaps more surprising was that Madoff had managed to run the Ponzi scheme for decades without getting caught. In the wake of the high-profile case, forensic investigators have been left asking themselves whether there were any clues that could have alerted them to the scam earlier.

There is evidence that ordinary organisations are also falling victim to fraud. According to a recent report published by the Association of Certified Fraud Examiners, fraud accounts for US$6.3 billion in losses globally, with the typical firm losing up to 5% of its revenues to fraud annually.

What is forensic accounting?

It has become increasingly important for organisations to take steps to detect fraud, and accountants can play a key role in doing so. Forensic accounting is an area of accounting that engages in the investigation of an organisation's records for evidence of financial crimes, including fraud. Forensic accountants seek to detect evidence of fraud, misconduct, and other regulatory violations by carefully examining data from an organisation using both quantitative and qualitative techniques. Traditionally, forensic accountants have had to rely on manual processes in conducting their investigations. This often involves meticulous and tedious reviews of accounting documents to identify suspicious transactions and records. Since even the most insignificant records can represent evidence of fraud, all records have to be painstakingly reviewed and scrutinised.

Using technology to detect fraud

In their recent article examining how technology can be used in forensic accounting, Lem Chin Kok and Elisa Ang from accounting firm KPMG highlight that digitisation "provides more data points that may constitute evidence, hence more opportunities to detect instances of fraud, misconduct and non-compliance. Investigator techniques and approaches have changed along with the digitisation of the environment we live in."

However, with a recent survey by KPMG finding that only 3% of fraud is currently being detected using fraud-focused analytics, there is scope for firms to leverage technological advances to intensify their use of analytical techniques in fraud detection. According to Delena Spann, an expert in fraud analytics, there are five common categories of fraud analytics approaches to detecting fraudulent activities:

i.   First, rules-based analytical approaches detect fraud by identifying known behaviours that fraudsters commonly exhibit in committing specific fraudulent activities and seeking to uncover these behaviours when they occur. Such analytical techniques help identify abnormal transactions or data, drawing attention to these instances for further investigation.

ii. Second, anomaly detection analytical techniques identify abnormal patterns in aggregated data that do not conform to established normal behaviour. Any abnormal patterns identified in the data are indicators of potential fraud and are flagged for further investigation by fraud investigators.

iii. Third, predictive modelling analytical techniques involve the statistical analysis of current and historical data to assess or predict future behaviour. To the extent that predicted behaviours differ from actual behaviours, fraud investigators should examine the reasons for these differences in behaviours and establish if they are due to fraud.

iv. Fourth, recent improvements in machine learning technologies have allowed fraud investigators to rely on neural networks — a form of unsupervised learning based on historical data — for the purpose of identifying unknown patterns which may be indicators of fraud.

v.   Fifth, visual analytics techniques seek to establish graphical representations of relationships and correlations found in data.

Visual analytics techniques represent a powerful way in which fraud investigators can design analytical procedures to detect fraud.

Detecting fraud using Benford's law

Would the analytical techniques have been effective in detecting fraud like the one that was being perpetuated by Bernie Madoff? Interestingly, a simple analytical test, designed based on the relatively obscure Benford's law, could have pointed investigators to the Madoff fraud even before it began to unravel. Benford's law gives the expected frequencies of digits in tabulated data. For example, the law provides that, in a randomly generated set of data, numbers should have one as their first digit about 30.1% of the time. This expected frequency then decreases progressively for digits two to nine, with numbers expected to have nine as their first digit only about 4.6% of the time.

A Ponzi scheme, like the one ran by Madoff, often falsely leads investors to believe that profits derive from an underlying business when it in fact generates returns for early investors simply by using investments from new investors to pay profits to older investors. Accordingly, any profits or returns disclosed by a Ponzi scheme are likely to be fabricated because no real underlying business actually exists. If data on profits or returns were fabricated, they would then not be likely to obey Benford's law.

Consistent with this, digital analysis performed to compare the frequencies of the first digits of the monthly returns from 1990 to 2008 of Fairfield Sentry Fund — one of Madoff's largest feeder funds — with expected frequencies based on Benford's law shows substantial anomalies in the monthly returns reported by the fund (with average deviations of about 3%), consistent with fraudulent activity.

Conclusions

In the face of the ever-growing threat of fraud, organisations need to develop robust methods of detecting fraudulent activity. As we enter the digital age, and with the accounting industry becoming increasingly reliant on technology, forensic accountants must develop forensic analytical techniques that allow them to examine large volumes of data expeditiously to effectively detect anomalies, patterns, and trends that may be indicative of fraud.

Part 1 of this chapter was first published on 27 February 2017 by CFO Innovation under the title "Are You Ready? Data Analytics is Reshaping the Work of Accountants."

Part 2 of this chapter was first published on 6 March 2017 by CFO Innovation under the title "Continuous Auditing: A New Instrument in the CFO's Toolbox."

Part 3 of this chapter was first published on 15 January 2020 in The Business Times under the title "Forensic Accounting Must be More Robust."

6

Digital Transformation in Healthcare SMEs

Background

The healthcare industry is plagued with systemic inefficiencies creating issues for patients, doctors, hospitals, insurance companies, employers, and governments across Asia. Some of the challenges include access to primary healthcare, accountability, cost, quality, information exchange, and utilisation of services. Unfortunately, the healthcare industry has historically been deliberate and measured in responding to changes and has lagged behind with digital transformation. This chapter elaborates on why the future lies in digital technology for the healthcare industry. In particular, it explores the trends in the modern healthcare landscape, which include the emergence of telehealth and on-demand healthcare, wearable technology, big data, and virtual reality. More importantly, for many healthcare small and medium-sized enterprise (SME) owners, the ultimate question will be as follows: How can they increase their digital capability?

Why Digital Transformation is Necessary for the Healthcare Industry

Driven by technological advances, digital transformation has been reshaping the global economy at a breakneck speed and transformed the world in which we live. Conventional notions about how businesses are structured; how firms interact with each other and with their customers; and how consumers seek and obtain services, information, and goods have been upended. No industry is spared. From the way we work, shop, do our banking, and play, almost everything can be done digitally through a handheld device. Businesses can now reach and connect with more customers than ever before. According to a study by Google, Temasek, and Bain & Company on e-commerce in Southeast Asia, some 40 million new users in the region joined the internet in 2020.[1]

With just a few taps and swipes of their mobile device, today's highly connected consumers can have what they want, where and when they want it. As the world becomes more digitally connected, and the on-demand economy further accelerates, the opportunities and challenges are enormous. Businesses in every industry will have to cater to these "right now" consumers or risk missing out on enormous opportunities. The healthcare industry is no exception.

With the disruptive dynamics and digital technologies being unleashed into the industry, incrementalism will not work anymore. Now more than ever, healthcare companies need to digitally transform. The COVID-19 pandemic has taught us that if the business is not digital, it is no longer in business. From government services to gyms and from retail to restaurants, companies regardless of size were forced to pivot to a digital model overnight.

Even as they grapple with the "here and now" urgency of managing their businesses, digital transformation is no longer a matter of choice for healthcare SMEs. According to Dr. Tedros Adhanom Ghebreyesus, Director-General, World Health Organisation, "The future of health care is digital."[2] To remain relevant and thrive in the future economy, healthcare SMEs need to transform digitally to be a digital business.

SMEs in the Healthcare Industry

Healthcare SMEs play an important role in the delivery of primary care in most countries in Asia. In Singapore, 80% of the primary healthcare

[1] https://www.bain.com/globalassets/noindex/2020/e_conomy_sea_2020_report.pdf.
[2] World Health Organization, "Leveraging telehealth for efficient delivery of primary health care in the WHO South-East Asia Region", https://apps.who.int/iris/handle/10665/350199.

needs are met by about 1,800 general practitioner (GP) clinics.[3] These are mainly solo practices or medium-sized groups and are not very efficient in the delivery of their services. In other parts of Southeast Asia, a growing middle class, a fast-ageing population, and increasing awareness of healthcare are stressing the healthcare systems. The traditional model of healthcare delivery is thus no longer sustainable. Disruption by digital platforms is inevitable.

For healthcare SME owners, this digital on-demand economy has created another layer of challenges for them to operate in. The role of an SME owner has always been a challenging one. They have to be hands-on in managing the day-to-day operations and activities of the business and, at the same time, monitor and respond to new opportunities and threats from the ever-changing environment.

Digital can bring many benefits to SMEs if it is properly aligned with its strategy and the needs of its end customers. Rushing headlong to become more digital is not going to solve the problem or give the SME a competitive advantage. Instead, it may create more confusion and trip them up in the process.

Many SME owners understand the need for the digital transformation of the business. But, the capabilities vary across the health SME community, and keeping up with digital transformation can feel overwhelming. Many struggle with the "How" questions: How can I digitally transform and future-proof my business? How much will it cost? How do I get started when I don't know much about technology?

Digital and Digital Transformation

The terms "Digital", "Digitisation", "Digitalisation" and "Digital Transformation" are sometimes used interchangeably, but they mean different things. For some, it's about the adoption of new technologies. It's about platforms, cloud-based systems, social media and application programming interfaces (APIs). For others, it means engaging with customers through digital channels

---

[3] Ministry of Health, Primary Healthcare Services, https://www.moh.gov.sg/home/our-healthcare-system/healthcare-services-and-facilities/primary-healthcare-services.

and means. And for others still, it represents a transformation of their way of doing business: a transformation of their business model. These definitions are not necessarily incorrect. But such diverse perspectives do little to help the already confused SME owners resulting in piecemeal initiatives or misguided efforts that lead to missed opportunities or wasted investments.

Before SME owners embark on their digital transformation journey, it's important to start with a clear understanding of exactly what digital transformation means and how their businesses may be transformed through digital.

According to Gartner's IT Glossary, "Digitisation is the process of changing from analogue to digital form".[4] Digitisation is essentially about taking something non-digital and converting it into a digital format so that it can be stored, processed, and transmitted digitally. For instance, scanning a paper document and saving it as a digital file (e.g., PDF or JPEG).

Digitalisation, however, refers to the leveraging of digital technologies and digitised data to enable or improve existing processes. What it does is that it converts a human-driven process into a software-driven process. For example, instead of having the nurse manually check the temperature and blood pressure level of every patient every hour, instrumentations are installed to monitor each patient at a pre-determined frequency and to automatically update the system. Digitalisation increases productivity and efficiency while reducing costs by improving how the work is done. But, it does not change or transform the work itself.

Digital transformation is the reimagining of the business and involves the leveraging of digital technologies to create new or modify existing business models, processes, and customer experiences to meet the ever-changing customers' needs. It pays to bear in mind that digital transformation is more than just the adoption of the latest technology.

Mindset Determines the Results

Digital transformation begins first with how you think about, and engage with, customers. A growth mindset is critical. The first thing that needs

---

[4] https://www.gartner.com/en/information-technology/glossary/digitization.

to change is the mindset towards digital. As companies move from paper to spreadsheets to smart applications, digital transformation allows them the opportunity to reimagine how they do business, how they engage with their customers, and how to future-proof their business.

A study by ANZ Bank suggests that SMEs have four different mindsets on digitalisation: the Digitally Advanced, the Digitally Confident, the Digitally Tentative, and the Digitally Dismissive. Depending on the mindset of the SMEs, it leads to different approaches being adopted and different results.[5]

Companies with a Digitally Advanced mindset have a robust understanding of digitalisation as well as their internal capabilities to leverage the benefits of digitalisation. They are found to have the highest use of digital tools and were thus able to derive strong value from their investment in digital.

Companies with a Digitally Confident mindset are found to have relatively good adoption of digitalisation. This stemmed largely from their beliefs in the benefits of digital transformation. However, they have yet to fully realize their full potential due to integration challenges.

Companies with a Digitally Tentative mindset are found to have a relatively high usage of digital tools. However, they are not realising the full potential of digital due to ineffective adoption and integration of digital tools in their business. They had to rely heavily on external help to increase their digital capabilities.

Last, but not least, are companies with a Digital Dismissive mindset. Due to their lack of internal digital knowledge and capability, Digitally Dismissive companies are sceptical about the benefits of digitalisation. As a result, they have low confidence in exploring digital technologies.

Comparing the Digitally Advanced with those having a Digitally Dismissive mindset, the study found that arising from the use of digital tools, Digitally Advanced companies saw a 44% increase in the average revenue per employee per year and more than double the hours saved per week.

---

[5] ANZ Bank, The Digital Economy: Transforming Australian Businesses, https://media. anz.com/content/dam/mediacentre/pdfs/mediareleases/2018/August/ANZ%20The%20 digital%20economy%20web.pdf.

Modern Healthcare Landscape

To digitally transform the business, healthcare SME owners need to have a view of the evolving healthcare landscape. A combination of manpower shortage, a fast-ageing population, and rapid technological advancement is driving change in the healthcare system in Asia. Medical technology, through early detection tools and up-to-date monitoring, can support the prevention of chronic diseases, injury, or other conditions, as well as in treatment selection and acceleration of recovery. The benefits are better health and quality of life. Some of the major developments include the following:

1. Telehealth and On-demand Healthcare

Today's connected consumers live in an on-demand economy that delivers instant gratification. They can have what they want, when they want it, with just a few taps and swipes of their mobile device and wherever they happen to be.

As patients seek on-demand healthcare, the healthcare industry must be able to respond to the demand through teleconsulting and wearable medical devices or risk missing out on the opportunities. Advancements in integrated computer and telephony (ICT) technologies and 5G mobile technologies are making these all possible now. Alternative care settings (which include home health and virtual health) are expected to roughly double over the next 10 years. The benefits include better and more efficient primary care delivery and higher customer satisfaction. In addition, it frees up capacity in the hospitals.

Furthermore, in Asia, where many patients live far from healthcare providers and facilities, by leveraging digital and telephony technologies, teleconsulting can bridge the gap and ensure quality primary healthcare is delivered to those who would otherwise not be able to access it.

2. Wearable Technology

Wearable technologies, such as Apple Watch and Fitbit, are getting increasingly sophisticated and come with heart rate monitors, exercise trackers, oximeters, and ECG. Gone are the days when all our health and medical records are kept by the doctors and hospitals. These days, all our health information resides on our wrists. Wearable technology allows consumers to take better care of their health. Wearable technology can also provide remote and regular monitoring of high-risk patients to determine the likelihood of a major health event. Preventive measures can be taken before the occurrence of a major health event. The Big Tech companies, such as Apple and Google, are muscling in on this opportunity. Healthcare SMEs can collaborate with the Big Tech firms to capture the opportunity.

3. Big Data in Healthcare
The aggregation of data available through various sources helps healthcare companies to identify patterns and trends. Big data in healthcare can provide several benefits. For example, big data can facilitate preventive care and better management. Big data analysis and predictive models could help identify potential health risks in people and create preventive or mitigation plans to keep them healthy and out of hospitals. Predictive modelling could be utilised to help hospitals and clinics estimate future admission rates, better manage their staffing and resource needs, as well as understand the developmental paths of illnesses and diseases and what will develop to become major problems in the future.

4. Virtual Reality in Healthcare
Treating patients with virtual reality is no longer science fiction. From pain management to honing the skills of medical professionals, virtual reality is fast changing the treatment of patients. The benefits include a reduction in cost and errors, an improvement in the quality of treatment, and the training of medical professionals.

How Can SMEs Increase Their Digital Capability?

For many SME owners, digital transformation can feel overwhelming for them. Developing a digital strategy and executing it require skills that are not within their core competencies.

The approaches SMEs can take to increase their digital capabilities differ depending on the mindset of the SME owners.

- For the Digitally Dismissive SMEs, there is little value in jumping in blindly. Given their lack of internal digital knowledge and capability, and their scepticism about the benefits of digitalisation, they need to start by taking small steps to understand and test the value of digital strategy and what it can provide to their business. Digitally Dismissive SMEs should engage with service providers that can provide tailored expertise to help them develop a digital strategy and take the first step.

- The challenge for the Digital Tentative SMEs is different from that of the Digitally Dismissive. They have experienced some mixed success, which can tilt either way. Inevitably, some of the digital projects may not turn out as expected. Building the confidence of the team and persevering in the digital journey is critical. Having a set of well-defined objectives, providing training to the staff to raise awareness, and discussing the value they may deliver and what they need to do to make implementation a success are crucial first steps. Digitally Tentative SMEs should also consider engaging external expertise to help in refining their digital strategy and develop their digital capabilities.

- The Digitally Confident SMEs have a good grasp of the changing digital environment and have developed an understanding of their digital options and their abilities. They have experienced some successes in their experimentation with digital. The next step would be to scale up. Identifying ways to continue to develop their digital expertise and embedding it as a core competence, exploring the relevance of emerging technologies, and integrating digital strategy as part of their overall business strategy is key in the next stage of development.

- The Digitally Advanced SMEs have enjoyed good successes with their digital strategies. They have built it as one of their competencies and have seen uplifts in both revenue and productivity. The journey does not end here. The Digitally Advanced SMEs will have to continue to create an internal culture and harness their digital curiosity for growth. A regular review and assessment of the relevance and outcomes of their digital strategy and alignment with their overall business strategy are needed to stay ahead of the ever-changing environment.

Conclusions

Digital transformation is posing an existential threat to companies that are not able to respond. To remain relevant and thrive in the future economy, healthcare SMEs need to transform digitally to be a digital business.

To transform digitally, however, is not about having the latest technologies. Digital transformation requires a reimaging of the business model, how the company thinks about and engages with customers, and how to future-proof the business. It starts with having the right mindset, having a well-defined digital strategy, and taking the necessary steps to learn and implement it. The mindset determines the digital dividend.

Potential implementation challenges could include employees who may lack the necessary digital skills, resistance to change, and budgetary constraints. Training, professional help, and government assistance schemes are available to assist SMEs in their transformation journey. Notwithstanding the challenges, healthcare SMEs may face along the digital transformation journey, the benefits, and opportunities that it brings are enormous and will help future-proof the business.

This chapter is contributed by Dr. Patrick Tan, Senior Lecturer at the Lee Kong Chian School of Business of the Singapore Management University.

7

Digital Transformation in Logistics SMEs

Introduction

2020 had been extraordinary in general, given how the COVID-19 pandemic had both battered and transformed the global and Singapore economies. This chapter presents a case study of how a logistics small and medium-sized enterprise (SME) in Singapore is able to pivot itself to embrace the challenge of uncertainty due to the pandemic as well as the massive increase in e-commerce transactions and the emergence of new business opportunities, which resulted in a many-folds increase in demand for logistics services. In particular, this chapter also outlines the various investments in digital technology that the company has already made, starting back in 2012, to be at the forefront of technology and the leader in digital transformation in the logistics industry in Singapore.

Case Study: XDel Singapore Pte Ltd

The company was initially known as "H & D" when it was first set up in 1993. "H" stood for "Harold [Lee]", who was the Managing Director of XDel Singapore, and "D" was the initial of his then partner. It was subsequently renamed "XDel", which was short for "Express Delivery", to better reflect the nature of its business. XDel Singapore was involved in express courier and delivery services, as well as e-commerce and last-mile fulfilment, international and cross-border deliveries, and mailroom and logistics activities.

From a two-man operation in 1993, XDel Singapore had grown its staff strength to close to 100 as of 2021. Its vehicle fleet of vans and motorcycles is numbered around 65, while its revenue had risen to S$7.2 million in 2020 from S$35,000 in its first year of operations.

The company had previously won the Top Five Prominent Award at the SME One Asia Awards 2012 and the Singapore Prestige Brand Award 2014 from the Association of Small & Medium Enterprises (ASME) and local Chinese daily *Lianhe Zaobao*. As for Harold himself, he picked up his first award in 2004 from Spirit of Enterprise, and subsequently, he also bagged The Entrepreneur of the Year Award (EYA) in the Established Entrepreneur category in 2016 from Rotary Singapore-ASME.

Services offered

XDel Singapore's delivery services gave customers the option of choosing either the time by which their items would be delivered on the day they were sent out or the duration of the delivery job from the time the item was picked up from the sender until the time it reached the recipient.

If they chose the first option, items could be delivered by 4.30 pm or 5.30 pm on the same day, or 5.30 plus. Choosing 5.30 plus meant that XDel Singapore had the flexibility to deliver the items to the recipient by 5.30 pm or latest by the next working day before 12 pm. For the second option, the items could be delivered within 1.5, 2.5, or 3.5 hours of sending them out, depending on the customer's preference, with an additional option of after office hours, which were from 6 to 10 pm.

The company's e-commerce and last-mile fulfilment services included end-to-end fulfilment from warehousing to "pick and pack" and API integration, which was essentially XDel Singapore customising its system to fit the client's needs and specifications such that both XDel Singapore and the client's information technology (IT) systems could "communicate" with each other seamlessly. Meanwhile, XDel Singapore's mailroom and logistics services enabled its clients to run their mailrooms with reduced manpower as a result of its IT-powered solutions. As for its international and cross-border deliveries, XDel Singapore worked with FedEx and United Parcel Service (UPS) to also offer end-to-end fulfilment and API integration.

XDel Singapore's marketing tagline was "Delivering Simplicity", which meant that beyond the items it was hired to deliver, it sought to offer both the sender and recipient a fuss-free experience as far as possible.

Cost structure

XDel Singapore's cost structure was primarily value-driven, but elements of the cost-driven approach were present. Although it did not outsource the services it offered, it did seek to automate many of its activities so that its staff could focus on providing better service to its customers. For instance, rather than conduct manual route planning, the company had chosen to tap on an automated route planning software that it licensed from Singapore's Agency for Science, Technology and Research (A*STAR),[1] which could guide its couriers to the location they needed to get to.

XDel Singapore also did not hide the fact that its services were not the cheapest but opted instead to provide clients greater value, such as through API integration, which was only possible because it had an in-house IT team to attend to such customisation requests. Other courier companies that bought IT solutions off the shelf would not be able to conduct this kind of customisation, just like it was not possible to add more drawers to a ready-made cupboard.

As with all businesses, XDel Singapore's cost structure comprised a combination of fixed and variable costs. The former included rent and staff salaries, while the latter largely came from fuel costs for its vehicles and utility costs incurred to provide its services.

Revenue streams

The firm predominantly derived its earnings from usage fees for its various delivery-related services. These were mainly recurring revenues although non-frequent users of its services provided a certain level of transaction-based revenues. Other than customers who chose to engage XDel Singapore's services on a regular basis, clients that opted for API integration were obliged to offer the company a stipulated volume of business. While these

---

[1] A*STAR, a statutory board under the Singapore Ministry of Trade and Industry, was the country's lead public sector research and development agency.

clients are not charged for the integration service, as part of the agreement to do it for them, they must offer XDel a certain business volume. The benefit offered by such an integration is that the likelihood of customers switching to another vendor due to reasons like price is reduced.

XDel Singapore is also thinking of franchising the business to Third World countries since it had already incorporated a considerable amount of business and technological know-how into its courier business to further diversify its revenue streams.

Key Technological Innovations Developed In-House

To enable the company to better scale the productivity ladder, XDel Singapore's IT team came up with its HOMES Enterprise Resource Planning (ERP) System.[2] With this system, the company could conduct electronic billing and do billing by account, address and contact levels, as well as by cost centre. In addition, it could support complex billing algorithms, and algorithms that worked on attendance and courier salary calculation.

The IT team also developed a proprietary mobile app called LUKE. At first, it could track deliveries and the location of the couriers, but as more functionalities were incorporated into the app, couriers could call the recipient via LUKE using the VoIP function and transmit images taken as evidence that they had completed their jobs. XDel Singapore was believed to be the first courier firm in the local market to provide proof of delivery.

In order to offer its customers greater convenience, XDel Singapore further enhanced its website capabilities, such that it could create delivery jobs through the XDel Online Shipping Tool without having to call the company to order a delivery. They could also retrieve consignment notes and the proof of delivery for filing later on. Moreover, customers could use the Virtual Chat Service (VCS) function to chat with the company's customer service staff virtually via the XDel Singapore website in real time if it was not convenient to make voice calls. The VCS function was first introduced by XDel Singapore in 2007 before it became mainstream in recent years.

---

[2] ERP systems ran on software that organisations used to manage their day-to-day business activities like accounting, project management, and supply chain operations.

Gains from Long-Term IT Investments

Competitive advantage

Among the key reasons for justifying substantial investments in IT was that it would take XDel Singapore's rivals a considerable period of time to match or even replicate the company's proprietary software.[3] Back in 2012, XDel Singapore was already believed to be the only local courier company that could track deliveries, adjust delivery loads, and compare delivery performance in real time.[4]

At that time, at least S$500,000 had already been invested in XDel Singapore's IT infrastructure. Lee added that from 2012 to 2021, another S$1.5 million had been invested in IT, meaning that more than S$2 million had been poured into IT infrastructure building since the founding of the company.

The amount spent on IT might appear disproportionate for a firm of XDel Singapore's size, but the management was of the opinion that it needed to do business in a similar manner to large courier players, such as DHL, and this could only be accomplished through the extensive use of sophisticated technology.[5]

Significant improvements in efficiency and productivity

The investments in technology also translated into significant improvements in efficiency and productivity, particularly with the introduction of VoIP, the artificial intelligence-powered Springboard engine licensed from a government agency, and the use of messaging apps (WhatsApp followed by Telegram).

Although XDel Singapore's decision to switch to VoIP was fortuitous, since the customer service staff could work from home immediately when it was mandated by the government during the Circuit Breaker period

---

[3] "Harold Lee: XDel Singapore — Spirit of Enterprise Honouree 2004", *Spirit of Enterprise*, 2004.

[4] Clement Teo, "Tech Levels Playing Field for Courier Firm", *The Business Times*, August 13, 2012.

[5] "Harold Lee: XDel Singapore — Spirit of Enterprise Honouree 2004", *Spirit of Enterprise*, 2004.

from April to May 2020, the original intention was to enable XDel to better manage its customer service levels. This was because prior to the adoption of the VoIP system, they would receive complaints from customers from time to time about rude couriers and miscommunication. With this system, all phone calls the company received and made were recorded. These recordings thus provided concrete evidence for the management to investigate when complaints were received. Staff could also learn what not to do or say based on the real-life examples gathered from the recordings.

In addition, because the VoIP system is plugged into HOMES, the management can now track the number of calls the customer service staff answered, the number of jobs they handled, and so on, so if there are any productivity issues, the management can zero in on these and tackle them as they arise.

Moreover, since these staff were working from home, they did not need to commute and could start serving customers earlier. In addition, they took turns to work from 6 pm to 9 pm to support the night delivery service, thus further improving XDel Singapore's productivity levels.

Ever since XDel Singapore started licensing the Springboard engine from a government agency as part of its Vehicle Route Planning (VRP) software, the company had been able to advise its couriers on which job to prioritise and the most effective routes to their destinations. XDel's couriers still retain the freedom to modify their routes according to their experience because the VRP system can sometimes lead them to take more convoluted paths. But if there are unforeseen mishaps, such as accidents along an expressway, the system is able to guide couriers to take an alternative route. At the same time, customer service staff would be alerted so that they can inform the affected customer about the delay.

The use of such advanced software had also made XDel Singapore's operations far more dynamic: new jobs could be added to a courier's job list as and when they were received such that the courier could collect and deliver a new item if in the vicinity. Otherwise, the courier could bring the item back to the office where the operations team would process and task it to another courier. This was possible as the VRP system could identify a courier's location based on the address of his delivery destination. Being able to estimate the duration between deliveries using the distance between successive delivery jobs also enabled the company to perform live monitoring of delivery progress, thus reducing the possibility of its couriers skiving.

With the WhatsApp messaging app gaining popularity in Singapore since 2011,[6] XDel Singapore's IT staff began exploring the idea of using it to facilitate communication between the various departments and also with XDel Singapore's customers. They found that it was a cost-effective method for everyone. When WhatsApp began charging companies for corporate usage, XDel Singapore's IT staff explored the option of switching to the Telegram app. This was found to be feasible, and the firm began using Telegram since 2018.

In addition, information, such as job status and daily staff strength, was also at the fingertips of the management through HOMES, which made monitoring and analysis efforts much easier (refer to Figure 1 for a chart on how HOMES has evolved over the years).

Powerful data analytics leading to better decision-making

Given that XDel Singapore collected considerable data on delivery activities performed by its staff, it could construct a heat map to identify the highest volume delivery areas for the day or hour for different types of customers. Such data analytics helped the company make better decisions about how it recruited and deployed people, as well as how it planned the routing for its delivery jobs and allocated jobs to its couriers.

Enhanced security for confidential documents for the customers

XDel Singapore offered an added level of security to customers that engaged it for deliveries involving important or confidential documents. For such deliveries, its IT staff would generate bar codes that encoded the delivery locations. In addition, the Android-based handsets that the couriers carried would be loaded with the company's mobile app, LUKE,

---

[6] Irene Tham, "SMS Usage Falls amid Rise of Chat Apps, Soft Tokens", *The Straits Times*, July 25, 2017, https://www.straitstimes.com/singapore/sms-usage-falls-amid-rise-of-chat-apps-soft-tokens.

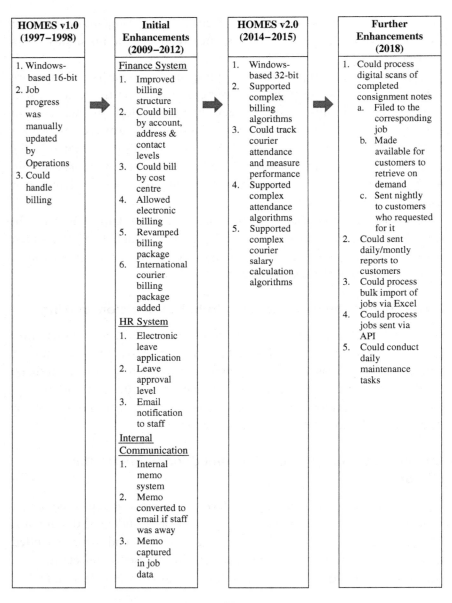

HOMES v1.0 (1997–1998)	Initial Enhancements (2009–2012)	HOMES v2.0 (2014–2015)	Further Enhancements (2018)

1. Windows-based 16-bit
2. Job progress was manually updated by Operations
3. Could handle billing
	Finance System
	1. Improved billing structure
	2. Could bill by account, address & contact levels
	3. Could bill by cost centre
	4. Allowed electronic billing
	5. Revamped billing package
	6. International courier billing package added
	
	HR System
	1. Electronic leave application
	2. Leave approval level
	3. Email notification to staff
	
	Internal Communication
	1. Internal memo system
	2. Memo converted to email if staff was away
	3. Memo captured in job data
		1. Windows-based 32-bit
		2. Supported complex billing algorithms
		3. Could track courier attendance and measure performance
		4. Supported complex attendance algorithms
		5. Supported complex courier salary calculation algorithms
			1. Could process digital scans of completed consignment notes
			  a. Filed to the corresponding job
			  b. Made available for customers to retrieve on demand
			  c. Sent nightly to customers who requested for it
			2. Could sent daily/montly reports to customers
			3. Could process bulk import of jobs via Excel
			4. Could process jobs sent via API
			5. Could conduct daily maintenance tasks

Figure 1.   Evolution of the Homes ERP System

Source: XDel Singapore.

which displayed the couriers' photos and QR (quick response) codes that recipients could scan to authenticate the couriers with their smartphones. Furthermore, all couriers, when on the job, were tracked via the Global Positioning System (GPS). Refer to Figure 2 for a chart on how LUKE has evolved over the years.

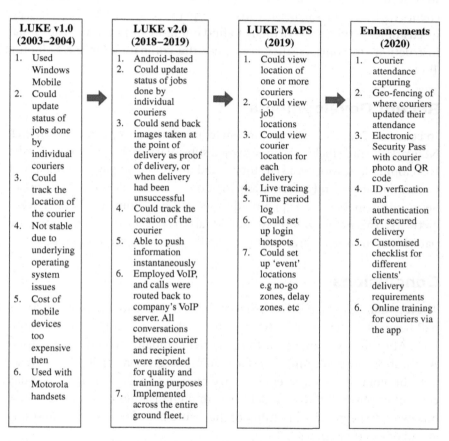

LUKE v1.0 (2003–2004)	LUKE v2.0 (2018–2019)	LUKE MAPS (2019)	Enhancements (2020)
1. Used Windows Mobile 2. Could update status of jobs done by individual couriers 3. Could track the location of the courier 4. Not stable due to underlying operating system issues 5. Cost of mobile devices too expensive then 6. Used with Motorola handsets	1. Android-based 2. Could update status of jobs done by individual couriers 3. Could send back images taken at the point of delivery as proof of delivery, or when delivery had been unsuccessful 4. Could track the location of the courier 5. Able to push information instantaneously 6. Employed VoIP, and calls were routed back to company's VoIP server. All conversations between courier and recipient were recorded for quality and training purposes 7. Implemented across the entire ground fleet.	1. Could view location of one or more couriers 2. Could view job locations 3. Could view courier location for each delivery 4. Live tracing 5. Time period log 6. Could set up login hotspots 7. Could set up 'event' locations e.g no-go zones, delay zones. etc	1. Courier attendance capturing 2. Geo-fencing of where couriers updated their attendance 3. Electronic Security Pass with courier photo and QR code 4. ID verfication and authentication for secured delivery 5. Customised checklist for different clients' delivery requirements 6. Online training for couriers via the app

Figure 2.   Evolution of the Luke Mobile App

Source: XDel Singapore.

Customer empowerment to track delivery progress

XDel Singapore had also developed ways for customers to track the progress of a delivery job without needing to call its customer service staff for updates. They could check the delivery progress on the XDel Singapore website using their account numbers and the job numbers. However, if clients wished to be further involved in the process, such as chatting with its customer service staff virtually to find out more or providing additional instructions to couriers, they could use the company's Online Shipping Tool.

Recent Developments

In February 2021, XDel Singapore had entered into an agreement with Pick Network Pte Ltd (Pick), a wholly owned subsidiary of the Infocomm Media Development Authority, a statutory board under the Singapore Ministry of Communications and Information, to be one of a selected group of Logistics Service Providers (LSPs) appointed to serve the Nationwide Parcel Locker Network. This network allowed individuals to collect their online purchase parcels anytime at a conveniently located locker station managed by Pick.

Conclusions

The top management of XDel believed that XDel Singapore's tech-savviness had been a key factor in enabling it to be selected as an LSP to work with Pick. After all, not many of the local courier companies could boast of their Application Programming Interface (API) integration capability. Even so, as technological advancement marched on, would XDel Singapore one day run out of physical things to deliver with digitalisation becoming the new buzzword? The firm had to think of the future in order to survive and stay ahead of its competitors.

Going international had always been part of the plan for XDel Singapore. China, in particular, had been identified as one of the possible markets the company was interested in venturing into, since it was the world's largest goods exporter. It used to deliver e-commerce shipments for Alibaba's Taobao e-commerce platform. However, this has since ceased as the company did not find it profitable to engage in it further.

In that case, which other fields should XDel zero in on next, and which industry in China should they start off with, if not e-commerce? These are strategic decisions that the top management of XDel will continue to ponder upon as the company enters the post-pandemic world with optimism.

This chapter is adapted from the Singapore Management University (SMU) Teaching Case titled "XDel Singapore: Using Technology to Deliver Simplicity", published by the SMU Centre of Management Practice in June 2021.

8

Digital Transformation in Microfinance SMEs

Background

Chapter 4 has provided a roadmap that small and medium-sized enterprises (SMEs) can use to navigate when they are interested in using Artificial Intelligence and Data Analytics (AIDA) in their digital transformation journey. This chapter features a case study of how a Myanmar-based microfinance lending start-up, Daung Capital, used AIDA techniques to manage its credit risk challenges.

Myanmar

Myanmar is the second-largest country in Southeast Asia in terms of landmass. The densely forested, largely rural country is located between India and Thailand. Following its independence from the British in 1948, the country experienced prolonged fragility from 1962 to 2011. During this time, an oppressive military junta wielded absolute power in the face of international censure and sanctions resulting in decades of economic stagnation, mismanagement, and isolation.

It was only in 2011 when political reforms started to come into effect that measures were adopted to overhaul the economy and reintegrate it with the rest of the world. A managed float of the Burmese Kyat was established in 2012. The Central Bank was granted operational independence in July 2013. In September 2013, a new anti-corruption law was enacted. However, Myanmar was still predominantly an agricultural economy. Despite the reforms, the country faced severe economic challenges in dealing with issues, such as inadequate infrastructure, underdeveloped human resources, and insufficient access to capital. The (2015–2016) global competitiveness index of the World Economic Forum had ranked Myanmar at 131 out of 140 countries that had been analysed in the survey and had identified access to finance as the primary factor for its low ranking.

As of 2017, access to financial services was severely limited in Myanmar. More than 75% of the adult population did not have access to formal financial services, and only 2% of the population owned a debit card (compared to 26% in Indonesia and 55% in Thailand). Most of the population relied on informal financial services, such as payday lenders and pawnshops, who often charged exorbitant rates. Moreover, a challenging legal and regulatory environment as well as corruption and a lack of transparency were considered the top constraints for doing business in Myanmar.[1]

Microfinance in Myanmar

Microfinance institutions (MFIs) were an essential way to provide access to financial services to the population of Myanmar. Between 2012 and 2017, MFIs had become increasingly prevalent, with 168 licensed MFIs operating in the country due to the microfinance law passed in 2011 that allowed local and foreign investors to establish privately owned MFIs in the country. Research had estimated that MFIs operating in Myanmar served an estimated 1.45 million clients, out of which 85% were women, with a total loan portfolio of approximately US$200 million. The sector included several prominent international NGOs and development organisations, such as the United Nations Development Fund (UNDP), Accion, and World Vision's Pact Global Microfinance Fund (PGMF), the oldest and largest MFI in Myanmar, which dominated the microfinance sector in the country, serving approximately 750,000 clients with US$125 million in loans. Despite PGMF's dominant position in the market, there was healthy competition and growth amongst other MFIs in the country. Notably, the non-performing loan rate for MFIs in Myanmar was extraordinarily low. Most loans were made to groups rather than individuals. Cultural

---

[1] Removing Barriers to Doing Business Key for Myanmar's Growth, The World Bank, https://www.worldbank.org/en/country/myanmar/publication/investment-climate-assessment-in-myanmar.

factors, such as people not wanting to be in debt in the future or be a burden on their families with debt, and intense social pressure to repay, forced people to pay back their loans on time and in full. Most MFIs were based in developed areas of the country like Yangon, Mandalay, and Ayeyarwady. MFIs avoided operating in smaller towns and villages, as the more remote regions required higher operating costs (given the lower population densities), and there was a lack of reliable infrastructure and communication networks.

Although the rise of private sector MFIs was helping to increase access to financial products and services for the poor in Myanmar, there were several challenges that needed to be addressed in order to scale up and drive higher financial inclusion. One major constraint was that MFIs were prevented from using voluntary deposits as a source of financing loans. Foreign-owned MFIs could only borrow from foreign lenders, who preferred to lend in US dollars. Moreover, foreign lenders were unreliable and hard to get, and securing loan approvals from the central government was a tedious and time-consuming process. Local MFIs could only borrow from local banks, which loaned in Kyat.[12] The local banks also demanded physical collateral, namely land, to secure a loan, yet few MFIs had any land to pledge for such a loan. At the same time, foreigners were not allowed to own any assets in Myanmar. As a result, the MFI sector in Myanmar was growing slower than was possible, and demand remained largely unmet.

Finally, another major challenge was the lack of information sharing between MFIs to check the creditworthiness of borrowers. The absence of a credit bureau, resulting in the lack of reliable data, was an additional issue. Increased competition between MFIs had also reduced the incentive to share information about clients among MFIs, which indirectly encouraged borrowers to take out multiple loans from different MFIs, leading to over-indebtedness.

Despite the challenges, Myanmar presented tremendous opportunities for microfinance to act as an enabler in reducing poverty, creating sustainable economic progress and driving overall wealth creation. Myanmar's microfinance scene was nascent but rapidly developing. According to the International Monetary Fund, there were 176 MFIs in Myanmar (101 local agencies, 26 NGO/INGOs and 49 partnerships) in 2018, with a capital totalling US$420 million available to 2.7 million people.

Government regulations passed in 2016 and 2017 to support laws related to microfinance had helped catalyse the development of the microfinance sector. This upward momentum was partly due to the Myanmar Financial Inclusion Roadmap (2014–2020) initiative, where one of the targets was to increase formal financial inclusion to 40% by 2020.

The favourable government support and the relatively nascent market had motivated the founders of Daung to set up business in Myanmar amidst a growing MFI market. However, the real inspiration for Qiu to establish the company had come from a reflective moment.

Daung Capital

Daung Capital was set up in 2017 with the vision of helping the poor by three friends: Leon Qiu, Wang Yi Yen, a tax consultant from Singapore, and Mike Than Tun Win, who was already an established Burmese entrepreneur. It was initially a side business for Qiu, as he continued to work full time as a private banker. However, the three founders soon realised that there was a growing demand for microfinance in Myanmar, and Qiu quit his full-time job to concentrate on the business and focus on raising money from private clients and investors. Yen took up the role of CEO and relocated to Myanmar. He became the local anchor and drove deals with agencies and factories in rural and semi-urban areas to chart out loan disbursement plans. Win helped implement the technology vision and saw through the execution of the projects.

To begin with, Qiu and his friends applied for an MFI license to operate their microlending business in Myanmar legally. From the regulatory perspective, Myanmar had established policies for companies operating as microfinance institutions. A joint operational agreement was also established for Daung to act as a subsidiary of a non-banking entity. Qiu was able to raise investment from Singapore-based venture capital firm Majuven and a Burmese venture capital firm established by Win. In its Series A round of funding, Daung was able to raise US$12 million. Within two years of establishment, Daung transformed itself from a budding start-up to a profitable company. From 2018 to 2019, the company's revenue almost tripled with its vehicle rental-purchase scheme generating the bulk of its revenues (refer to Figure 1 for Daung Capital revenue, 2017–2019).

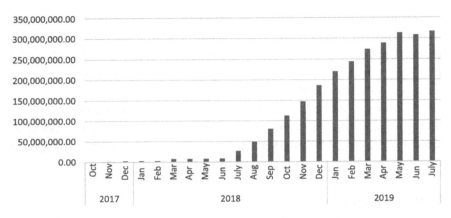

Figure 1.   Daung Capital Revenue (2017–2019)

Source: Company Data.

Lending Model

Daung's loan schemes were based on a Business to Business to Consumer (B2B2C) lending model. The company did not work with the customer directly but through dealers, factories and SMEs. Dealers and SME/factory partners comprised motorcycle renting and selling agencies, factories, small businesses and educational institutes. The MFI had several loan products of which two were the most prominent: motorcycle loans and cash advances to salaried workers.

Loans for motorcycles

In Myanmar, mobility was a crucial prerequisite for escaping poverty. Labourers could earn far more per day if they could travel outside their village on an everyday basis. Since public infrastructure did not support such frequency to commute, the poor were left to their own means to resolve the challenges they faced. Demand for motorbikes was high in Myanmar as they provided the much-needed mobility to the poor. An average working-class individual in Myanmar earned about US$300 per month with little to no savings, but a motorbike could cost at least US$263 — a difficult purchase for a low-income labourer. To help workers planning to buy motorcycles, Qiu and his team came up with a rent-to-own model (RTO), offering those with low incomes the possibility of owning a piece of machinery that could change their fortunes, allowing them to take up work in nearby towns and villages where they could commute daily.

Daung worked with motorcycle dealers across the country to give end customers immediate access to a motorbike with a small deposit. The RTO model offered low monthly repayments (typically from six months to a year), with protection against loss and damage incurred due to accidents during the loan period. At the end of the contract, upon full loan repayment, the ownership of the vehicle was transferred to the customer, with the customer receiving the owner book as proof of ownership.

Loans to salaried workers

Another scheme that Qiu and his team designed was to offer cash advances to salaried workers. Individual loans in Myanmar came with high-interest rates, a massive impediment to regular borrowing for low-income workers in factories. Interest rates for personal loans were set at 10% by the Central Bank of Myanmar and capped at 13%. Since 2019, individuals without collateral were allowed to borrow from banks but at an interest rate of 16%. Interest rates for personal loans were even higher through informal financial services, with local lenders and loan sharks charging up to 60% per month. Low-income salaried workers were often unable to get formal loans due to the lack of having collateral. Even without the need for collateral, borrowers were sceptical about applying for loans from formal financial services, due to the lack of trust. Qiu and his team studied this gap in the market and designed their personal loan product such that it could be easily accessible and affordable to the end customers and was disbursed in partnership with the factory they worked for, eliminating trust issues. They also introduced a dynamic interest rate instead of a fixed interest rate for individual borrowers.

Factors such as monthly income, repayment period and borrowed amount were key to rate calculation. Using the company's online loan calculator tool, individuals could calculate the interest rate that would be charged for a specific amount that they wanted to borrow. For example, if a worker had a monthly wage of US$300 and an intent to borrow US$600 with a repayment period of 12 months, the monthly payment instalment would amount to US$62 and the total repayment would amount to US$744. The interest rate was roughly 1.24% — much lower than the average rate of 2.5% charged by other MFIs. The duration of loan payment was flexible, and borrowers could choose six months, 12 months, or 18 months. Qiu and his team collaborated with the factories to execute such loan products as a service for the workers. The monthly payment amount was deducted from the salary of the worker directly every month.

Tangible Strategies for Combating Risk

The main objective behind microfinance was simply the provision of financial services to those excluded from the formal financial system. Since eliminating poverty was a long-haul journey, an ideal microfinance program was expected to keep offering its services over time. Sustainability of a microfinance establishment was, therefore, key to its effectiveness in attaining its objectives over the long run. The likelihood that borrowers might not pay the money back (plus interest) was perceived to be the most common and often most serious vulnerability for an MFI. Since most microloans were unsecured, credit risk associated with such loans was higher — delinquency/default could very quickly multiply from a few cases to a large percentage of the portfolio.

This contagious effect was further provoked by the distribution of microfinance portfolios that tended to have a high concentration in certain business sectors. Consequently, many clients could be exposed to the same external threats, such as the lack of demand for client products, livestock disease outbreaks, bad weather and many others. These factors could create volatility in microloan portfolio quality, heightening the importance of controlling credit risk. In this context, MFIs required a monitoring system that could highlight repayment problems clearly and quickly so that loan officers and their supervisors could focus on delinquency before it got out of hand. Managing risks in a lending business was absolutely key to business sustainability. A critical factor in a lending model was the risk-adjusted return, which could determine the sustainability of the model in the long run.

Managing the risk of a loan portfolio, therefore, required "skin in the game" of all parties involved, especially the microfinance organisation, to enable the execution of a sound lending scheme. Several failures in microfinance pointed to the premise that MFIs could ideally only trust a counterparty, a vendor (especially in a frontier economy) when everybody shared both the upside and downside risks. Qiu and his team understood the importance of "skin in the game" in the lending business and devised their lending model accordingly to ensure that risk was distributed across the value chain amongst all parties.

Examples of failed microfinance organisations were widespread. In India, for instance, many MFIs were struggling due to a lack of initiatives in managing credit risks. For example, in the Indian state of Andhra Pradesh, a microfinance crisis emerged in 2013, when lenders were not able to repay their loans. MFIs in the state started adopting harmful recovery practices, which in turn further aggravated the issue. Frustrated by the bad harvest and harassment from MFI lenders, many borrowers committed suicide. The tragic incidents affected not only the microfinance industry but also the overall finance sector in the country.

As microfinance was still a new practise amongst the rural population of Myanmar, Daung's target end customers had little understanding of loan schemes offered by MFIs. In addition, there were other key challenges in credit risk management in Myanmar, including the absence of a credit bureau, and the low availability and reliability of financial statements of agent and dealer organisations. Qiu and his team had to come up with innovative ways to combat credit risk. One way to deal with credit risk was to operate through partnerships wherein the credit risk of the loans could be partially diffused. In addition, the loan duration was short (a few months); hence, the overall risk of non-repayment was lower. Qiu and his team were also experimenting with implementing a formal credit risk assessment methodology to help them better manage credit risk as they expanded their customer base.

Motorcycle loans

For the motorcycle loans, Daung had two contractual agreements: one with the dealer and another with the borrower. Daung did not bear the risk of the borrower not paying back; the dealer actually takes that risk. However, Daung needed eyes on the end borrower to make sure that it did not fund motorcycles that do not exist or borrowers that do not exist. To implement such monitoring, it depended on technology. For most buyers, such a purchase is usually their first formal loan, and hence the propensity to pay back is higher — the willingness to pay is high. Moreover, the agents we deal with filter the customers they are comfortable extending the loan to, who have a steady source of income and will be able to repay over a few months.

Relying on procedures and systems for loan disbursements, such as a digital scan of the resident permit and thumbprint, allowed Daung to create a database of its borrowers and retain customer profile information. Profile information was also helpful in granting subsequent loans to the customers for other needs in the future, like buying a refrigerator or a kettle.

The tracking of the loan repayment at Daung's end was done through technology-based solutions. The customers would submit their instalments in cash every month at the dealer's place. To submit the instalment, they had to log in to a tablet app at the dealer's location and provide their thumb imprint for verification. The dealer would then transfer the collected cash electronically to Daung's account to avoid risks arising from cash transfer through physical means.

Salary loans

For disbursing loans to salaried people, Daung collaborated with well-known factories with large staff strength (of more than 100 workers). Qiu and his team also chose organisations that had an international reputation (like a factory of H&M or Zara), as they felt that this helped counter some credit risks. They also used the salary deduction model, as opposed to workers paying their loans back in cash instalments. Loan instalments were directly deducted from the worker's salary and transferred electronically to Daung. Again, the contracts for the loans were made both with the factory and the individual borrower. One filter was that borrowers had to be employees, and another was to cap the maximum monthly deduction to 50% of the worker's salary. Individuals reneging on their loans was a small risk. If a worker is fired or changes company, Daung restructured the loan and waited for the worker to pay it back. However, the main risk is the possibility of the factory shutting down or going bankrupt. That was the more significant risk. Therefore, Daung was very cautious in choosing its partners. Its loan capping is based on the World Bank ethical lenders guidelines.

Other loans

In line with Daung's mission of empowering the communities it served, the company had also launched a scheme to finance Tuk-Tuks (auto-rickshaw), in collaboration with Myanmar-based ride-hailing company: Get Ride. Daung had also launched a loan scheme to grant education loans to students from low-income families, in collaboration with institutes that provided professional courses.

New loan scheme: Harvesting farmer loans

In 2019, Qiu and his team ventured into a new customer category, which was virtually barred from the formal financial system due to its peculiarities. They stumbled upon the idea of the new product by chance when extending a loan to a rice mill. Farmers in rural Myanmar typically sold their produce to rice mills during the harvest season and received payment based on their produce. However, only farmers who could afford high-quality seeds had a large harvest and hence a better price for their produce. Farmers bought their seeds from the rice mill but often had to turn to loan sharks for loans to buy them. After paying off their hefty debts, they typically had little money left, even in a good harvest year. Qiu decided to design a loan product for the farmers that would enable them to buy high-quality seeds from the rice mill at a low-interest rate and repay the loan after harvesting. Keeping the harvest cycles in mind was crucial in designing the loan product.

There were mainly three different avenues for farmers to access credit formally: MFIs, financial cooperatives, and the Myanmar Agricultural Development Bank (MADB). Going to MADB for a loan was quite common; nevertheless, the bank's loans were designed with only the rice farmer in mind. The loan scheme provided by MADB offered loans to farmers at the rate of US$100 per acre, capped at a maximum of US$1,000. However, the loan scheme had two major issues in the way it was structured. First, the cost of producing rice per acre was higher — an average of US$150 per acre. Second, the loan was issued after the seed-sowing period with a loan term that was due just after harvest time. This instigated a vicious cycle of borrowing, forcing farmers to take loans from other sources to pay back the agricultural loans. Existing MFI loan schemes, on the other hand, required frequent repayment (sometimes bi-weekly). Such constraints had triggered more informal lending habits amongst farmers.

Harvests in Myanmar were driven by wet and dry seasons. Conventional Burmese crops were rice, corn, beans, and pulses. Rice and corn were grown during the monsoon season, while beans and legumes were cultivated during the dry season. For rice, there were two sowing seasons: one in the monsoon season, which was harvested from late October to November, and another in the summer, which was harvested in late March. The income of farmers was tied to the harvest periods.

The saving habits of farmers were unique in their own right. Most farmers saved little, preferring not to keep their savings in cash but to invest in gold. Myanmar also had low crime rates in rural areas, hence keeping reserves in gold was not considered risky. Moreover, farmer families were religious, mostly Buddhists. They donated small amounts to their local monasteries, believing that such good deeds would help them in their "afterlife". Most farmers depended on loan sharks for making seed purchases, and gold was the most common form of collateral for easy loans.

All harvest buyers (including rice mills) had natural incentives (the prospect of better earnings) to promote a good quality harvest and did their best to support farmers to acquire good quality seeds, crop supplies, and labour. Despite such arrangements, farmers often failed to produce a good quality crop, as harvests could be affected by unforeseen shocks, bad weather or pest infestations. Fluctuations in market prices of crops and bad weather influenced farmers, forcing them to pre-sell or abandon a crop or to even choose to migrate to cities to find other work. A poor harvest due to late rain or pest infestation affected not only the farmers but also the labourers they employed. Financial recovery from a bad crop year could take as long as six years for a farmer to overcome.

Moreover, farmers often needed supplementary capital, compelling them to pre-sell their paddy at about 70% of the harvest market price. As a result, the farmer rarely saw the full return on his investment and the profit for the full worth of his paddy. Despite recent adjustments to the loan structure by MADB for payback timing, there was still a significant discord.

A new loan product, therefore, presented opportunities that could assist the farmer in maximising profits and adjusting his access to capital (by selling at off-peak times when the market price was higher). Moreover, what was required was a loan scheme that had payback terms which coincided with the farmer's harvest cycle.

Daung saw a gap in the loan market for farmers and designed a loan scheme for farmers that would enable them to borrow money for their seeds and maybe machinery for their farms at affordable interest rates. If Daung could run the loan scheme in collaboration with rice mills, it could reduce the risk of non-payment by asking the mill owners to deduct the loan amount from the farmer's harvest proceeds.

As November was rice harvest season in Myanmar, Qiu and his team decided to launch their farmer-loan product at that time, as it would allow farmers to get to know about the scheme before the seed-buying period for their next harvest. Having the rice mill implement a buy-back clause for the harvest ensured that farmers would pay back their loans diligently. The rice mills also benefitted, as they were able to motivate more farmers to buy good quality seeds, which would lead to better harvests.

Pertinent issues

Although Qiu and his team had been able to establish Daung as a socially responsible for-profit business in Myanmar, there were several challenges and uncertainties that they still faced in their day-to-day operations. While microlending institutions had expanded rapidly over the last few years in developing economies, they were increasingly proving to be unsustainable over the long run. Operational inefficiencies were not uncommon, and only charities with no profit-making goals had been able to continue due to their nature of operations, as working under losses was not an issue for them as long as there was sufficient funding. Under these circumstances, Qiu wondered if Daung could run its loan schemes efficiently over a long period. The greatest challenge by far was to disburse and collect loans in a sustainable manner.

Even though Myanmar was a primarily rural, developing economy, the outreach of mobile phones in the country had reached spectacular levels in the recent past. The mobile penetration rate in the country was 110%, and more than 50% of the population had access to smartphones as of 2018. Such mobile penetration ratios indicated the possibility of creating mobile-based products to reach out to the hitherto inaccessible rural communities. However, despite the high mobile penetration rate, the digital media literacy rate amongst the populace was low. Farmers in Myanmar didn't access Google; they went to their mobile agent and asked the service personnel at the agency to download Facebook for them for a small price. They then used Facebook search for looking up addresses and finding other information, and this is the only social media they use.

Given the backdrop, MFIs like Daung had to design their products and services across such unique characteristics of their target end customers. One pertinent issue is how could Daunh ensure that the new loan product for farmers met all their needs. More importantly, could Daung mitigate the credit risks that arose from executing such specialist products for the low-income populace? Daung could consider implementing risk management processes to ensure the sustainability of its business. Alternatively, it could use avant-garde technology, such as advanced data analytics and machine learning, to monitor and spearhead the implementation of credit risk processes more effectively.

Conclusions

Established in 2017 by Leon Qiu and two other co-founders, Daung had grown in the past two years to expand its business to reach thousands of low-income customers in Myanmar, all of whom had limited access to formal financial products and services. In 2019, Qiu and his team were laying the final groundwork for their new service product launch. The product was a microfinance loan scheme for farmers in rural Myanmar and was one of a kind in the market. Qiu and his team had pondered over the various constraints around which the loan product for farmers needed to be constructed. Careful credit risk assessment of the target customer base was a critical criterion in designing the product. Ethical obligations and decision-making were essential considerations as well.

9

Developing Skillsets and Capabilities to Drive Digitalisation in SMEs Acquisition of Digital Skillsets — Optimisation and Simulation

One key factor which determines the success of an accounting organisation's digital transformation efforts relates to the digital skills that accountants possess. In particular, even as accountants need to possess expertise in the accounting domain, they increasingly also need to be proficient with digital skillsets which allow them to implement and work with technology. This chapter highlights and illustrates how the following two analytical techniques can be used by accountants to approach and solve common problems faced in the accounting and finance setting: (i) Optimisation and (ii) Simulation.

Part 1: Optimisation Skills

Goal programming was introduced as a branch of multicriteria decision analysis. It has been applied for decision-making in many areas, including in accounting, resource planning, energy forecasting, and many others. The key elements in a goal programming model include the following:

- **Decision variables**: The values of decision variables are often unknown at the start of the problem. These variables usually represent things that a manager can control, and his/her goal is to find values of the decision variables that best satisfy stated goals.
- **Goals**: These represent targets which a manager wishes to achieve. Goals are viewed as "soft constraints" (i.e., a constraint which is preferred but not required to be satisfied). A manager would often have to make trade-offs among different goals to determine an acceptable solution to a goal programming problem.
- **Goal constraints**: Constraints are mathematical functions that incorporate decision variables to express limits on possible solutions. Goal constraints are a particular type of constraint which allows a manager to determine how close a given solution comes to achieving stated goals. In stating goal constraints, deviational variables are introduced to represent the amount by which each goal deviates from its target value. In particular, negative deviational variables represent the amount by which each goal's target value is underachieved and positive deviational variables represent the amount by which each goal's target value is overachieved.
- **Hard constraints**: Not all constraints in a goal programming problem have to be goal constraints. Hard constraints set conditions for decision variables which must be satisfied.
- **Objective function**: The objective of a goal programming problem is to achieve all the goals as closely as possible. An objective function expresses a manager's corresponding goal of minimising the weighted sum of percentage deviations from stated goals. Weights are assigned to deviational variables in an objective function to reflect the importance and desirability of deviations from the various goals.

Implementing a Goal Programming Model in a Spreadsheet — An Example

This section illustrates how goal programming can be implemented on a spreadsheet and used to solve decision problems using an example relevant to management accountants:

Atlas Co. is a manufacturer of metal casings for computers. The company has recently hired a consultant to advise it on its plan to purchase new machines to expand manufacturing capacity. Based on the space available in Atlas' manufacturing plant, the consultant suggests that Atlas should *ideally* purchase five small machines, 10 medium machines, and 15 large machines. Each small machine can produce 400 units of metal casings per day, while each medium machine can produce 750 units of metal casings per day and each large machine can produce 1,050 units of metals casing per day. The company also learns that it would be ranked among the largest manufacturers of metal casings in the city if its new machines can produce 25,000 units of metal casings per day. This would be a key marketing point for the company and would be helpful when negotiating new contracts with customers. It will cost US$18,000 to purchase a small machine, US$33,000 to purchase a medium machine, and US$45,150 to purchase a large machine. Atlas has allocated a tentative budget of US$1,000,000 to purchasing these new machines. Atlas must decide how many small, medium, and large machines to purchase based on these facts.

Atlas can structure the above facts as a goal programming problem to help it make its purchasing decision. In this goal programming problem, Atlas has the following five goals:

1. The purchase should include *approximately* 5 small machines.
2. The purchase should include *approximately* 10 medium machines.
3. The purchase should include *approximately* 15 large machines.
4. Together, the new machines should produce *approximately* 25,000 units of metal casings per day.
5. The new purchases should cost *approximately* US$1,000,000.

Figure 1 presents the goal programming problem mathematically. The decision facing Atlas is the number of small, medium, and large machines to purchase. This is represented by the decision variables X_1, X_2, and X_3, respectively. The objective function in the problem seeks to minimise the weighted sum of percentage deviations from stated goals. Goal constraints utilise negative and positive deviational variables, represented by d_i^- and d_i^+,

Minimise:

$$\frac{1}{5}\left(w_1^- d_1^- + w_1^+ d_1^+\right) + \frac{1}{10}\left(w_2^- d_2^- + w_2^+ d_2^+\right) + \frac{1}{15}\left(w_3^- d_3^- + w_3^+ d_3^+\right) + \frac{1}{25000}\left(w_4^- d_4^- + w_4^+ d_4^+\right) + \frac{1}{1000000}\left(w_5^- d_5^- + w_5^+ d_5^+\right)$$ } Objective function

Subject to:

$X_1 + d_1^- + d_1^+ = 5$ } Small machine goal constraint

$X_2 + d_2^- + d_2^+ = 10$ } Medium machine goal constraint

$X_3 + d_3^- + d_3^+ = 15$ } Large machine goal constraint

$400X_1 + 750X_2 + 1{,}050X_3 + d_4^- + d_4^+ = 25{,}000$ } Total daily production goal constraint

$18{,}000X_1 + 33{,}000X_2 + 45{,}150X_3 + d_5^- + d_5^+ = 1{,}000{,}000$ } Total budget goal constraint

$d_i^-, d_i^+ \geq 0$ for all i constraint   } Deviational variables hard

$X_i \geq 0$ for all i

X_i must be integers   } Decision variable hard constraint

Where

X_1 = number of small machines to purchase

X_2 = number of medium machines to purchase

X_1 = number of large machines to purchase

Figure 1.   Atlas' Goal Programming Model

	A	B	C	D	E	F
1	Problem Data	Small Machine	Medium Machine	Large Machine		
2	Production Quantity	400	750	1,050		
3	Purchase Cost	18,000	33,000	45,150		
4						
5	Constraints	Small Machine	Medium Machine	Large Machine	Production Quantity	Budget
6	Actual Amount				0	0
7	Under Achieve					
8	Over Achieve					
9	Goal	0	0	0	0	0
10	Target Value	5	10	15	25,000	1,000,000
11						
12	Percentage Deviation					
13	Under Achieve	0.00%	0.00%	0.00%	0.00%	0.00%
14	Over Achieve	0.00%	0.00%	0.00%	0.00%	0.00%
15						
16	Weights					
17	Under Achieve	1	1	1	1	1
18	Over Achieve	1	1	1	1	10
19						
20	Objective	0.000				
21						
22						
23	Decision variables					
24	Objective function					
25	LHS of constraints					

Figure 2.   Atlas' Goal Programming Problem Implemented on a Spreadsheet

respectively, to allow a manager to determine how close a given solution comes to achieving his/her stated goals.

Next, the mathematical goal programming model is implemented in an Excel spreadsheet. Figure 2 presents the spreadsheet model used, while Table 1 presents the formulas used in the spreadsheet.

X_1, X_2, and X_3 (in the mathematical model) represent the *decision variables* (i.e., how many of each machine to purchase) and are represented in cells B6, C6, and D6, respectively. The values of these decision variables are unknown at the start of the problem. There are five goals, related to the number of small, medium, and large machines to buy, to daily production quantity, and to the overall budget, which Atlas wants to achieve. These goals are represented in cells B10, C10, D10, E10, and F10, respectively. Atlas' stated goals also form part of the goal constraints in the goal programming problem, specifically, the goals form the right-hand side of each corresponding goal constraint. The left-hand side of the goal constraints allows the manager to measure the extent to which specific goals are achieved and are represented in the spreadsheet in cells B9, C9, D9, E9, and F9. In the spreadsheet, the objective function is represented

Table 1.   Formulas Used in Excel Spreadsheet

Cell	Formula
E6	=SUMPRODUCT(B6:D6,B2:D2)
F6	=SUMPRODUCT(B6:D6,B3:D3)
B9	=B6+B7−B8
C9	=C6+C7−C8
D9	=D6+D7−D8
E9	=E6+E7−E8
F9	=F6+F7−F8
B13	=B7/B$10
C13	=C7/C$10
D13	=D7/D$10
E13	=E7/E$10
F13	=F7/F$10
B14	=B8/B$10
C14	=C8/C$10
D14	=D8/D$10
E14	=E8/E$10
F14	=F8/F$10
B20	=SUMPRODUCT(B13:F14,B17:F18)

in cell B20. The objective function seeks to minimise the weighted sum of percentage deviations from stated goals. Negative percentage deviations from each goal are represented in cells B13, C13, D13, E13, and F13, while positive percentage deviations from each goal are represented in cells B14, C14, D14, E14, and F14. Weights assigned to each negative deviational variable are represented in cells B17, C17, D17, E17, and F17, while weights assigned to each positive deviational variable are represented in cells B18, C18, D18, E18, and F18.[1]

Having implemented the goal programming model in a spreadsheet, proceed to use the Solver function in Excel to find a solution to the problem. Solver is an add-in function in Excel that must be installed separately before it can be installed.[2] The Solver perimeter inputs used in

---

[1] In this example, weights of 1 are assigned to all deviation variables.

[2] Once installed in Excel, go to Data → Analyze → Solver to run the Solver function.

Table 2. Solver Parameter Inputs

Menu Field	Input
Set Objective	$B$20, To: Min
By Changing Variable Cells	$B$6:$D$6,$B$7:$F$8
Subject to the Constraints	$B$9:$F$9 = $B$10:$F$10
	$B6:$D$6 >= 0
	$B$7:$F$8 >=0
	$B6:$D$6 = integer
Select a Solving Method	Simplex LP

the example are presented in Table 2. In Solver, we need to define three key components of our spreadsheet model. First, we need to define an objective cell (and whether its value should be maximised or minimised). This cell corresponds to the cell in the spreadsheet that represents the *objective function* in the mathematical model. Second, we need to define variable cells. These cells should correspond to cells in the spreadsheet that represent *decision variables or deviational variables* in the mathematical model. Third, we need to define constraints. These cells should correspond to cells in the spreadsheet that represent both goal constraints and hard constraints in the mathematical model. Given that the objective and constraint functions in our goal programming problem are linear in nature, we use the "Simplex LP" method as the solving method in Solver.

Once these input perimeters have been defined, click "Solve" to instruct Solver to solve for a solution that minimises the objective function. Figure 3 presents the Solver solution to my example. Solver solves for the number of small, medium, and large machines that Atlas should purchase by minimising the objective function, given the set of weights assigned to the deviational variables in the problem. The spreadsheet indicates that Atlas should purchase five small machines, 10 medium machines, and 15 large machines.

Revising the Goal Programming Model

In goal programming, decision makers have to examine a given solution and evaluate if the extent to which individual goals are met or missed is acceptable. For example, the solution obtained in the previous section

	A	B	C	D	E	F
1	Problem Data	Small Machine	Medium Machine	Large Machine		
2	Production Quantity	400	750	1,050		
3	Purchase Cost	18,000	33,000	45,150		
4						
5	Constraints	Small Machine	Medium Machine	Large Machine	Production Quantity	Budget
6	Actual Amount	5	10	15	25,250	1,097,250
7	Under Achieve	0	0	0	0	0
8	Over Achieve	0	0	0	250	97,250
9	Goal	5	10	15	25,000	1,000,000
10	Target Value	5	10	15	25,000	1,000,000
11						
12	Percentage Deviation					
13	Under Achieve	0.00%	0.00%	0.00%	0.00%	0.00%
14	Over Achieve	0.00%	0.00%	0.00%	1.00%	9.73%
15						
16	Weights					
17	Under Achieve	1	1	1	1	1
18	Over Achieve	1	1	1	1	1
19						
20	Objective	0.107				
21						
22						
23	Decision variables					
24	Objective function					
25	LHS of constraints					

Figure 3.   Solution to Atlas' Goal Programming Problem

would lead to Atlas exactly meeting its goals of purchasing five small machines, 10 medium machines, and 15 large machines. However, it would, at the same time, lead to Atlas missing its goals of being able to produce 25,000 units of metal casings per day and keeping to a budget of US$1,000,000. Specifically, the solution would lead to Atlas being able to produce 25,250 units of metal casings per day (exceeding its production quantity goal by 250 units per day) and requiring a budget of US$1,097,250 (exceeding its budget goal by US$97,250). If the decision maker is satisfied with the extent to which his/her goals are met or missed, he/she could then proceed to implement the solution obtained in the goal programming model in his/her decisions.

However, if the decision maker is not satisfied with the extent to which goals are met or missed, he or she could explore alternate solutions by assigning different weights to the individual deviational variables. In general, positive weights should be assigned to deviational variables that represent deviations that are undesirable, a weight of zero should be assigned to deviational variables that represent deviations that are neutral, and negative deviations should be assigned to deviational variables that represent deviations that are desirable. The magnitudes of positive/ negative weights assigned to deviational variables should be increased as the undesirability/desirability of deviations increases.

For example, if the decision maker is not satisfied with the solution obtained in the previous section (perhaps he/she may feel that, given the initial budget goal of US$1,000,000, the required budget of US$1,097,250 in the solution is excessively high), he/she may decide to increase the magnitude of the weight assigned to the positive deviational variable for the budget goal from 1 to 10 (in cell F18). This would indicate an increase in the undesirability of exceeding the budget goal relative to other goals. Figure 4 presents the solution to the goal programming problem incorporating this change in assigned weight.

In this revised solution, Atlas would purchase five small machines, 10 medium machines, and 13 large machines. It would be able to produce 23,150 units of metal casings per day. The purchase would require a budget of US$1,006,950. Using this set of weights would reduce the budget that Atlas would require from US$1,097,250 (in the initial solution) to US$1,006,950 (in the current solution). However, while Atlas would still

	A	B	C	D	E	F
1	Problem Data	Small Machine	Medium Machine	Large Machine		
2	Production Quantity	400	750	1,050		
3	Purchase Cost	18,000	33,000	45,150		
4						
5	Constraints	Small Machine	Medium Machine	Large Machine	Production Quantity	Budget
6	Actual Amount	5	10	13	23,150	1,006,950
7	Under Achieve	0	0	2	1,850	0
8	Over Achieve	0	0	0	0	6,950
9	Goal	5	10	15	25,000	1,000,000
10	Target Value	5	10	15	25,000	1,000,000
11						
12	Percentage Deviation					
13	Under Achieve	0.00%	0.00%	13.33%	7.40%	0.00%
14	Over Achieve	0.00%	0.00%	0.00%	0.00%	0.70%
15						
16	Weights					
17	Under Achieve	1	1	1	1	1
18	Over Achieve	1	1	1	1	10
19						
20	Objective	0.277				
21						
22						
23	Decision variables					
24	Objective function					
25	LHS of constraints					

Figure 4.   Revised Solution to Atlas' Goal Programming Problem

be able to exactly meet its goal of purchasing five small machines and 10 medium machines, it would now only purchase 13 large machines (two short of its goal of 15 machines). It would also only be able to produce 23,150 units of metal casings per day (1,850 short of its goal of 25,000 units of metal casings per day).

There is no standard procedure for assigning weights to deviational variables that will lead to optimal solutions. Instead, a decision maker follows an iterative procedure where he or she assigns a particular set of weights to deviation variables, solves the goal programming problem, analyses the solution obtained, refines the set of weights, and then solves the problem again. Often this process is repeated many times over before an acceptable solution is obtained. Indeed, goal programming does not provide a single best solution to a problem, rather the nature of goal programming involves making trade-offs among the various goals until a solution that gives the decision maker the greatest level of satisfaction is found.

Conclusions

Goal programming is a tool that can be used for multicriteria decision analysis. It is an especially important tool for management accountants who often have to make decisions that involve trade-offs among multiple goals. In this chapter, we introduce goal programming, demonstrate how it can be implemented using Excel's Solver feature, and illustrate its use through an example from management accounting. While this example is straightforward, it is representative of many decision-making problems faced by accountants in practice. In particular, it is reflective of many real-life scenarios which require accountants to make decisions while contending with multiple business goals (often in addition to other constraints).

Part 2: Simulation Skills

In Formula One, where races are often won or lost by margins of fractions of a second, the skill of the driver is as important as the race strategy devised by team strategists. While luck certainly plays an important part in the success of any race strategy, many other factors, such as fuel load, tire

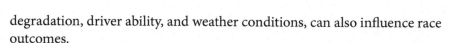

degradation, driver ability, and weather conditions, can also influence race outcomes.

To help them devise winning race strategies, F1 teams are increasingly turning to sophisticated simulators which can run thousands of race simulations while changing variables in each simulated race. By running numerous simulations, race strategists gain insights into likely race outcomes when different combinations of variable inputs are implemented, thus helping them devise the race strategy that would give them the greatest chance of success in the actual race.

Simulation is an extremely useful decision-making tool not only in F1 but also for accountants. While many companies have invested heavily in developing sophisticated software to help them run simulations, simulations can also be run on tools, such as Excel. In this section, we will use a simple example to demonstrate how an accountant could use Excel to run simulations.

Conducting Simulation in Excel

Simulation is a mathematical technique for solving a problem by performing a large number of trial runs (called simulations) and inferring a solution from the collective results of the trial runs. In simulations, uncertainty in a business situation is explicitly incorporated into a model via random variables.

In this example, we will look at Baker Limited, a fictitious insurance company which provides a health insurance plan to its customers. In particular, we examine how Baker can use a simulation model to determine how much money it should accrue in the coming year (2017) to pay for customer insurance claims.

It is now 31 December 2016. As of December 2016, Baker has 15,222 customers who each pay US$200 per month in premiums. Average insurance claim per customer in the month was US$185. Although Baker does not expect to raise premiums in 2017, it expects the number of customers signed on to the health insurance plan to increase by an average of 2% per monthand for average claims per customer to increase by an average of 1% per month. Figure 5 summarises these expected trends related to the insurance plan in 2017.

	A	B	C	D
1		2016	2017	
2		December	Assumptions	Rate
3	No of customers	15,222	Increasing	2%
4	Average claim per customer	$185	Increasing	1%
5	Premiums per customer	$200	Constant	

Figure 5. Summary of Expected Trends Related to the Insurance Plan in 2017

Any claims made by customers of the health insurance plan are paid out by Baker from premiums collected from other customers on the plan. Should premiums collected from customers be insufficient to pay claims, Baker would then have to pay these outstanding claims from its own cash account.

Baker needs to determine how likely it is that premiums collected will be able to cover claims made on this health insurance plan (i.e., that this insurance plan will be profitable) in 2017. If the insurance plan is likely to be profitable, Baker would not need to accrue any money to pay for customer claims (because they can be paid from profits). However, if the plan is not likely to be profitable, Baker would then have to determine how much money to accrue in order to pay for outstanding customer claims (from its own cash account).

Designing the Spreadsheet Model

A simulation model built on an Excel spreadsheet can be used to examine this problem. The first step in conducting a simulation in Excel is to develop a spreadsheet model of the business problem. Figure 6 presents the business problem modelled in a spreadsheet.

The following formulae are used in the spreadsheet:

Number of customers: In cell B10, the formula = B3*1.02 is used to determine the expected number of customers in January 2017 following a 2% increase from December 2016. In cell B11, the formula = B10*1.02 is used to determine the expected number of customers in February. This formula is then copied down to all cells in the column to determine the expected number of customers in the remaining months of 2017.

	A	B	C	D	E	F
1			Coming Year			
2		December	Assumptions	Rate		
3	No of customers	15,222	Increasing	2%		
4	Average claim per customer	185	Increasing	1%		
5	Premiums per customer	200	Constant			
6						
7						
8						
9	Month	Number of customers	Total customer contribution	Average claim per customer	Total claims	Company Profits
10	January	15,526	3,105,288	187	2,901,115	204,173
11	February	15,837	3,167,394	189	2,988,729	178,665
12	March	16,154	3,230,742	191	3,078,989	151,753
13	April	16,477	3,295,356	193	3,171,974	123,382
14	May	16,806	3,361,264	194	3,267,768	93,496
15	June	17,142	3,428,489	196	3,366,454	62,035
16	July	17,485	3,497,059	198	3,468,121	28,937
17	August	17,835	3,567,000	200	3,572,858	(5,859)
18	September	18,192	3,638,340	202	3,680,759	(42,419)
19	October	18,556	3,711,107	204	3,791,918	(80,811)
20	November	18,927	3,785,329	206	3,906,434	(121,105)
21	December	19,305	3,861,035	208	4,024,408	(163,373)
22						428,875
23						

Figure 6.   Details of Baker's Insurance Plan Modelled on a Spreadsheet

Total customer contribution: In cell C10, the formula = B10*200 is used to calculate total expected customer contributions (i.e., total premiums paid) in January 2017. This formula is then copied to all cells in the column to calculate the expected contributions in the remaining months of 2017.

Average claim per customer: In cell D10, the formula = B4*1.01 is used to determine the expected average claim per customer in January 2017 following a 1% increase from December 2017. In cell D11, the formula = D10*1.01 is used to determine the expected average claim per customer in February. The formula is then copied to all cells in the column to determine the expected average claim per customer in the remaining months of 2017.

Total claims: In cell E10, the formula = D10*B10 is used to calculate the expected total claims in January 2017. The formula is then copied to all cells in the column to calculate the expected total claims in the remaining months of 2017.

Company profits: In cell F10, the formula = C10−E10 is used to calculate the expected profits for the company in January 2017. The formula is then copied to the subsequent eleven cells in the column to calculate the expected profits for the company in the remaining months of 2017. In cell F22, the formula = SUM(F10:F21) is used to calculate the total expected profit for 2017. In Figure 6, we observe that the health insurance plan is expected to make a profit of US$428,875 in 2017.

Inserting Random Number Generators (RNGs) into the Model

In our spreadsheet model, we assumed that the number of customers signed on to the health insurance plan will increase at an average rate of 2% per month and that the average claim per customer will increase at an average rate of 1% per month in 2017. It is based on these assumptions that we determine that the insurance plan is expected to make a profit of US$428,875 in 2017 (as presented in Figure 6).

However, these growth rates are only estimates, and there is uncertainty over what the actual growth rates will actually turn out to be. Due to factors outside of Baker's control, there could be months where the growth rates exceed forecasted rates and other months where growth rates are lower than forecasted rates. An important step in spreadsheet simulation is to explicitly model uncertainty by placing a random number generator (RNG) formula in each cell that represents an uncertain outcome.

In particular, for each cell where an outcome is uncertain, an RNG formula will generate a value that represents a randomly selected value from a distribution of values that should mimic actual outcomes. In our example, although we specify an average monthly growth rate of 2% for the number of customers signed on to the insurance plan and an average monthly growth rate of 1% for the average claim per customer, there is uncertainty over what actual monthly growth rates will be. While average monthly growth rates over the year might indeed be 2% and 1%, respectively, it is likely that there will be some variations in monthly growth rates over the year.

In our example, let's assume that, even as average growth rates are 2% for the number of customers signed on and 1% for the average claim per customer, we expect these growth rates to follow the following distributions:

- **Number of customers**: Uniform distribution with discrete values from −3% to +7 (note that the average growth rate per month is still 2%).

- **Average claim per customer**: Uniform distribution with discrete values from –5% to 7% (note that the average growth rate per month is still 1%).

To model these uncertain monthly growth rates in our spreadsheet model, we would need to insert the following RNGs into our spreadsheet:

Number of customers: In cell B10, the original formula is replaced with = B3*(1+(RANDBETWEEN(–3,7))/100). This is used to calculate the expected number of customers in January 2017 given our expectation that the increase from December 2017 will follow a uniform distribution with discrete values from –3% to 7% (the RANDBETWEEN function in the formula generates discrete numbers randomly distributed between –3 and 7). In cell B11, the formula = B10*(1+(RANDBETWEEN(–3,7))/100) is used to determine the expected number of customers in February 2017. This formula is then copied down to all cells in the column to determine the expected number of customers in the remaining months of 2017.

Average claim per customer: In cell D10, the original formula is replaced with = B4*(1+(RANDBETWEEN(–5,7)/100)) to calculate the expected average claim per customer in January 2017 given our expectation that the increase from December 2016 will follow a uniform distribution with discrete values from –5% to 7%. In cell D11, the formula = D10*(1+(RANDBETWEEN(–5,7)/100)) is used to calculate the expected average claim per customer in February 2017. The formula is then copied to all cells in the column to determine the expected average claim per customer in the remaining months of 2017.

The spreadsheet model in Figure 7, which incorporates the relevant RNGs in the number of customers and average claim per customer columns, shows that Baker can expect to make a loss of US$2,474,011 based on this particular set of growth rates generated by the RNGs. Recalculating the model (press F9 to do so) will cause the RNGs to generate a different set of growth rates, leading to a different profit/loss scenario for Baker.

Running the Simulation

The next step in performing a simulation involves formally recalculating the spreadsheet model hundreds or even thousands of times (to generate a large number of "trial runs") and systematically recording the relevant

	A	B	C	D	E	F
1			Coming Year			
2		December	Assumptions	Rate	Distribution	
3	No of customers	15,222	Increasing	2%	Uniform distribution between -3% and +7%	
4	Average claim per customer	185	Increasing	1%	Uniform distribution between -5% and +7%	
5	Premiums per customer	200	Constant			
6						
7						
8						
9	Month	Number of customers	Total customer contribution	Average claim per customer	Total claims	Company Profits
10	January	14,765	2,953,068	196	2,895,483	57,585
11	February	14,913	2,982,599	208	3,099,904	(117,306)
12	March	14,466	2,893,121	204	2,946,769	(53,648)
13	April	15,044	3,008,846	198	2,972,701	36,145
14	May	15,345	3,069,022	204	3,123,119	(54,097)
15	June	15,652	3,130,403	218	3,408,572	(278,169)
16	July	15,339	3,067,795	218	3,340,401	(272,606)
17	August	15,186	3,037,117	220	3,340,067	(302,950)
18	September	15,641	3,128,230	209	3,268,255	(140,025)
19	October	16,423	3,284,642	215	3,534,618	(249,976)
20	November	17,573	3,514,567	224	3,933,323	(418,756)
21	December	17,221	3,444,276	239	4,124,483	(680,207)
22						(2,474,011)

Figure 7. A Profit/Loss Scenario for Baker's Insurance Plan Based on a Model Incorporating Relevant RNGs

outputs generated (the company profits for 2017). To do so, we will make use of the data table function in Excel. A data table is a range of cells (arranged in columns or rows) in which the values of specific cells can be changed in order to come up with different values for a problem.

Cells A26:B41 in Figure 8 show a small part of 1,000 replications carried out in our example. The data table generates these replications by systematically substituting values from cells A29 to A1028 into cell C28 and populating the corresponding cells in column B (from B29 to B1028) with the value that is calculated in cell B28. Accordingly, the data table causes the RNGs to generate 1,000 separate sets of number of customer and average claim per customer growth rates and thus allows our model to calculate overall company profits for each of these replications and to record them in cells B29 to B1028.

Analysis of Outputs

The output from the simulation is summarised in cells D26:E31 in Figure 8. Examining this information would be very helpful to Baker in

	A	B	C	D	E	F
7						
8						
9	Month	Number of customers	Total customer contribution	Average claim per customer	Total claims	Company Profits
10	January	15,222	3,044,400	178	2,703,427	340,973
11	February	15,831	3,166,176	183	2,895,911	270,265
12	March	15,356	3,071,191	183	2,809,034	262,157
13	April	15,202	3,040,479	188	2,864,372	176,107
14	May	16,115	3,222,908	200	3,218,408	4,499
15	June	16,759	3,351,824	210	3,514,502	(162,678)
16	July	17,262	3,452,379	203	3,511,339	(58,960)
17	August	17,780	3,555,950	207	3,689,012	(133,063)
18	September	17,958	3,591,509	222	3,986,716	(395,206)
19	October	19,215	3,842,915	215	4,137,812	(294,897)
20	November	19,599	3,919,773	205	4,009,540	(89,767)
21	December	20,775	4,154,960	217	4,505,119	(350,159)
22						(430,730)
23						
24						
25						
26	Data Tables for replication (1000 replications)			Parameters		
27	Replication	Company cost		Mean	345,370	
28		(430,730)		Standard Deviation	3,326,196	
29	1	(2,049,870)		Min	(11,831,095)	
30	2	3,254,500		Max	9,521,680	
31	3	1,687,787		Range	21,352,775	
32	4	(674,157)				
33	5	1,702,502				
34	6	(2,887,334)				
35	7	(1,537,068)				
36	8	1,623,532				
37	9	(497,307)				
38	10	(2,087,437)				
39	11	(115,369)				
40	12	520,971				
41	13	(6,467,217)				

Figure 8.   Extract of the First 13 Replications Carried Out in the Spreadsheet Model

understanding the potential profitability of its health insurance plan. For instance, while the mean profit for the 1,000 replication (or trial runs') is US$345,370, the simulation also indicates that there is a relatively large variance in the potential profitability of the health insurance plan given that the minimum recorded profits are –US$11,831,095 and the maximum recorded profits are US$9,532,680. Based on this information, Baker can then determine an appropriate amount of money to accrue to pay for outstanding claims.

Conclusions

As the example in this chapter demonstrates, careful analysis of the outputs obtained from simulation can greatly improve the insights available to decision makers and provides valuable information for decision-making, particularly in instances where outcomes of events that can influence outputs are uncertain.

Parts 1 and 2 of this chapter were first published in the Journal of Corporate Accounting and Finance. Part 1 appeared in Volume 30 (1), pages 161 to 168, while Part 2 appeared in Volume 29 (2), pages 133 to 138.

10

Developing Skillsets for Future Accountants

Background

The accounting profession is rapidly evolving due to technological innovations. Chapter 4 has highlighted how accounting organisations can approach digital transformation. Technologies, such as the Internet of things, smart sensors, cloud computing, robotics, and artificial intelligence, are combining to disrupt the way that businesses operate. It is predicted that, over the next decade, information technology (IT) will significantly transform the accounting profession. Certainly, it is clear that practitioners and academics in the accounting profession need to rethink about the future of the profession and take active steps towards embracing digital transformation. This chapter highlights two initiatives introduced by Singapore Management University's (SMU) School of Accountancy to equip accountants with relevant technology skillsets to be future-ready and help small and medium-sized enterprises (SMEs) in their digital transformation journey.

Part 1: SMU School of Accountancy Accounting Data and Analytics Second Major Programme

IT is expected to enhance transparency, accuracy, and the communication of financial information as well as offer opportunities for accountants to create value, perform more in-depth analyses, and provide timely financial advice. Some of the IT-enabled transformations in accounting will involve automation of not only mundane bookkeeping tasks but also complex, multifaceted processes including financial closing processes and fraud and forensic accounting. With the adoption of smart software and analytics that will enable better and near real-time reporting, the accounting profession expects that this will allow accountants to transition from retrospective to predictive analysis, and highlight the interconnectedness of financial and non-financial performance.

Although technological advances are set to transform the accounting profession in the coming years, there is a significant shortage of accounting professionals who possess the relevant skillsets to exploit these advances. To effectively leverage technology, accountants will need to develop new paradigms and skills. Within this regard, there have been calls for university programmes capable to equip accounting students with technology skills that they will bring to the future workplace.

Many employers have also shared their view that to better prepare students for the opportunities and challenges ahead, universities should infuse analytical exercises into existing curricula in order to help students develop proficiency in data and analytics, in addition to core accounting skills. Currently, firms are often forced to assemble two separate groups, one with expertise in accounting and the other with expertise in technology, to work together on complex issues requiring skillsets from both groups.

The Association to Advance Collegiate Schools of Business, also known as AACSB International, is a leading international accreditation body for university accounting and business programmes. It connects educators, students, and businesses to groom the next generation of great leaders. AACSB recommends that accounting degree programmes should include learning experiences that develop skills and knowledge related to the integration of IT in accounting and business. These experiences include the development of skills and knowledge related to data creation, data sharing, data analytics, data mining, data reporting, and storage within and across organisations. This is articulated in AACSB's International Accounting Accreditation Standard A7 (Information Technology Skills and Knowledge for Accounting Graduates).

Furthermore, the International Federation of Accountants also highlights that relevant skillsets, including those in IT, statistics, and data modelling, should be integrated into university programmes for both current and future accountants.

In Singapore, there has also been extensive discussion on the role of IT in accounting. For example, in 2015, the Singapore government established a committee on the future economy to develop economic strategies that can position the country well for the future. As part of the committee, a working group on legal and accounting services was formed. In its 2017 report, the working group acknowledged the role that technology will play in the jobs of accountants and recommended that universities should embed technology into the accounting and law curriculum. According to the Skills Framework for Accountancy published in 2020, digitisation and data analytics are among the core skills which will grow in demand as the accountancy sector continues to transform.

Consistent with these views, the Pathways Commission on Accounting Higher Education of American Accounting Association, a premier community of accountants in academia, highlights in its recommendation the need for universities to develop curriculum models, engaging learning resources and mechanisms for easily sharing them. Furthermore, the commission also notes that to achieve this, vital programmes, courses and approaches require systematic attention to curriculum, pedagogy, and opportunities for renewal. Specific objectives articulated to accomplish this recommendation include engaging the accounting community to define the body of knowledge considered to be the foundation for accounting's future curricula and implementing curricula models for the future.

In response to the call to prepare accounting graduates for digital transformation, SMU School of Accountancy (SOA) launched the Accounting Data and Analytics (ADA) Second Major programme in 2018 that students can pursue to complement their Bachelor of Accountancy degree programme.

The ADA programme is the first of its kind in Singapore. It aims to equip students with the relevant skills in data and analytics, which are in demand in the accountancy sector. This is particularly important considering that the need for accountants to become more tech-savvy and conversant with data has been identified as one of the important ways that can help the accounting profession continue to thrive amid digital transformation. Universities need to ensure that their accounting curricula meet these needs.

During the programme development phase, SOA conducted focus group discussions with 23 representatives of major employers of accounting graduates in Singapore to gain insights into the relevance of a programme in accounting data and analytics for the accounting profession. Specifically, 15 participants were from the Big Four accounting firms and held senior positions, such as audit partner, director, and chief information officer, while eight participants were from major financial institutions and held senior positions, such as head of finance and general manager of financial management.

Participants were supportive of the ADA programme and provided valuable insights. They agreed that accountants of the future should be exposed to new and emerging technologies that are relevant to the work of accountants. Participants commented that the following would form the core data technology skillsets required of accountants of the future: (i) Data management, (ii) data modelling and visualisation, and (iii) statistical tools/programming.

Curriculum Structure

Students need to complete eight courses to gain the ADA second major. The curriculum is designed based on three pillars: (1) Data technology, (2) analytics electives, and (3) accounting analytics capstone. The structure of the ADA programme is illustrated in Figure 1.

Students will take four compulsory courses under the data technology pillar to equip themselves with basic data and analytics skillsets useful for accountants. These courses include accounting information systems, business data management, data modelling and visualisation, and statistical programming.

In the second pillar, students will learn to apply these basic data and analytics skillsets by completing three electives courses. Electives available include forecasting and forensic analytics, analytics for value investing, audit analytics, auditing information systems, blockchain applications in financial services, and work-study elective.

Lastly, in the third pillar, students are required to apply the skills learned in the first two pillars by completing a compulsory accounting analytics capstone course. A key pedagogical innovation of the ADA second major

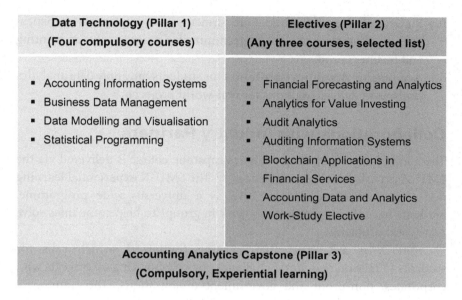

Data Technology (Pillar 1) (Four compulsory courses)	Electives (Pillar 2) (Any three courses, selected list)
<ul><li>Accounting Information Systems</li><li>Business Data Management</li><li>Data Modelling and Visualisation</li><li>Statistical Programming</li></ul>	<ul><li>Financial Forecasting and Analytics</li><li>Analytics for Value Investing</li><li>Audit Analytics</li><li>Auditing Information Systems</li><li>Blockchain Applications in Financial Services</li><li>Accounting Data and Analytics Work-Study Elective</li></ul>
Accounting Analytics Capstone (Pillar 3) (Compulsory, Experiential learning)	

Figure 1.   Curriculum Structure

is the compulsory accounting analytics capstone course that employs the unique award-winning SMU-X experiential learning pedagogy, which will be discussed in the following. Completing a capstone course helps students integrate and apply the knowledge, skills and abilities.

Learning Outcomes

The learning outcomes for the five compulsory courses are as follows:

(a) **Accounting Information Systems**: Our students can use data flow diagrams and system flowcharts to document business processes, analyse internal control weaknesses and recommend business process improvements.
(b) **Data Management**: Our students can apply data modelling techniques to design a database.
(c) **Data Modelling and Visualisation**: Our students can use appropriate modelling techniques to solve accounting and business problems.

(d) **Statistical Programming**: Our students can implement statistical analysis operations using a programming language to solve accounting and business problems.
(e) **Accounting Analytics Capstone**: Our students can apply data analytics skillsets to deliver solutions for real-world projects.

Collaborations with Industry Partners

The compulsory accounting analytics capstone course is delivered via the SMU-X experiential learning pedagogy. The SMU-X experiential learning pedagogy was introduced in 2015 as a university-wide programme. Students have the opportunity to work in groups to help companies solve real-world problems.

SMU-X is an experiential learning framework which calls for students to take on real-world challenges by collaborating on projects with corporates, non-profit and government organisations. The framework represents a paradigm shift in the traditional approach to teaching and learning; from being teacher-centred to active learning by students while working on the real-world problems. SMU-X also encourages instructors to collaborate closely with industry partners.

The SMU-X experiential learning pedagogy is built on four principles (see Figure 2).

Figure 2.   Four Principles of the SMU-X Experiential Learning Pedagogy

The four principles are as follows:

(i) **Project-based experiential learning**: combines academic with experiential learning through the heavy use of projects from industry partners;

(ii) **Interdisciplinary approach**: challenges students to use their knowledge and skills to tackle real-world problems through interdisciplinary approaches and activities;

(iii) **Active mentoring**: partners with corporate, non-profit and government-sector organisations. Industry partners and faculty are involved in active mentoring so that students benefit most from this collaborative relationship;

(iv) **Tripartite learning loop**: students get a better understanding of what it means to use theory learnt outside the classroom; faculty learn how real-world adapts theories; industry partners deepen their own learning through faculty and students' findings. This inculcates in our students, faculty and industry partners the value of continuous learning in a volatile, uncertain, complex and ambiguous (VUCA) world.

Through the SMU-X principles, the accounting analytics capstone course provides students with opportunities for active and collaborative learning, interactive experiences, access to subject-matter experts from academia and industry, and a deepened understanding of diversity and interconnectedness.

The following are three examples of industry projects completed by students during the compulsory accounting analytics capstone course.

Singapore Exchange (SGX)

SGX requested the students to devise a solution for their current revenue forecast process. The present system of SGX requires human intervention to manually sift through various new sources to determine the inputs for their forecast. This method may lead to higher chances of inaccuracy as significant human judgement is used to determine these inputs. The student group proposed converting the semi-automated revenue prediction process to a fully automated one in order to streamline the process and eliminate the human judgement bottleneck. This would enable a standard operating procedure, reduce total man-hours and improve the process accuracy over time.

Seng Hua Hng (SHH) Foodstuffs Pte Ltd

SHH requested the students to develop in-house data analytics capability to help the company achieve its strategic goals. Previously, SHH would rely on estimates to make key strategic decisions, such as determining annual production capacity. The key challenge of utilising estimates was the lack of accurate demand forecasting on a periodic basis and the absence of important financial information that would support the risk assessment of expansion into new foreign markets. The student group leveraged predictive analytics to find valuable insights, such as expansion plans for both domestic and overseas, new product introduction possibilities and better estimation of future financial targets.

XDel Singapore

XDel was struggling with payables-related issues. Previously, their finance department used manual processes, which were very time consuming and prone to errors. Due to the manual processes, there were certain issues, such as difficulties in reconciling payments, delayed payments to suppliers and non-payment to suppliers. The student group assisted their finance department to automate their processes. They also derived a formula for the company to calculate the cost per driver which they could implement in their cost management tool for better costings. XDel implemented the students' solutions and experienced a reduction in late and non-payments.

Increasingly, higher education has been called upon to train students to be more agile and capable of dealing with complex issues and systems at work. Therefore, there is a need for an education where students are rooted in content knowledge and be provided with hands-on learning that mirrors real-world problems, coupled with interdisciplinary work opportunities.

Work–Study Programme

Under the ADA second major programme, students can also opt for the Accounting Data and Analytics Work–Study Programme (WSP). Under this WSP, students will have the opportunity to undergo a 20-week extended internship at EY in Singapore across its service lines in assurance, tax, strategy and transactions, and consulting.

SMU aims to put in place work–study options where students may undergo longer internship durations to better interlace institution-based learning with structured on-the-job training and to facilitate more impactful work opportunities within the attachment company. This is another collaboration with industry partners besides the accounting analytics capstone course.

Before embarking on the extended internship, students are required to complete two courses (data modelling and visualisation, and business data management). During the extended internship, students will alternate between working four days at EY and studying on campus for one day each week. In contrast, students typically complete a full-time 8–10 week internship during their holidays. Through the 20-week programme, students will work on a data analytics project. Students will learn about the forms of data and how to analyse data and draw insights from it. Importantly, they will also gain exposure to and better understand how a professional services organisation like EY leverages data-driven insights to deliver exceptional service to clients.

Conclusions

The ADA programme is expected to benefit students by equipping them with relevant skillsets required for accountants of the future. Even as the accounting industry seeks to incorporate technology into its processes, there remains an acute lack of accounting professionals who possess the necessary technical skills required. As such, students who complete both a Bachelor of Accountancy degree and the second major in accounting data and analytics would be well placed to fill the "skills gap" that has developed in the accounting industry, thus improving their career prospects upon entering the industry.

Given the lack of accounting professionals who possess the necessary technical skills in the marketplace, employers can benefit from the ADA programme training accountants with key skills in data and analytics. Given the potential for technology to improve productivity and spur growth in the accounting profession, the hiring of accountants who also possess critical data and analytics skills to drive the implementation of technology would give firms a key competitive advantage over their competitors. A focus on incorporating data and analytics in accounting education is timely.

Part 2: Online Accounting Data Camp

Upskilling and life-long learning are two key phrases that then Education Minister Lawrence Wong highlighted in his speech at the Straits Times Education Forum 2021. The rapid emergence of digital technologies has disrupted many industries, including the accountancy sector. While accounting jobs will continue to exist and grow, the way that accounting work is carried out is no longer the same. Accounting functions are increasingly relying on digital technologies to enable their work. For instance, data analytics is deployed in audit and forensics to detect irregular patterns in accounting transactions. Machine learning algorithms are used to sharpen forecasting models to predict sales trends.

Such digital evolution in the accountancy sector has witnessed a growing call for "digital accountant": Accountants that are equipped with relevant digital knowledge and skillsets that allow them to handle and manipulate large quantum of data in daily accounting tasks and develop deep analysis in supporting business decision-making.

It is for this specific purpose of upskilling current accountants and preparing future accountants to embrace digital technologies that the School of Accountancy (SOA) of SMU launched its inaugural online data camp on "Digital Transformation & Financial Analytics" in late August 2020. The main objective of the camp was to provide participants with basic knowledge of accounting and data analytics, and programming skills in Python. At the same time, participants also get an opportunity to experience SMU's interactive teaching pedagogy, a hallmark of SMU's undergraduate as well as postgraduate education.

A major challenge encountered in organising the data camp was the COVID-19 pandemic. With the prohibition of face-to-face lessons owing to safe distancing rules, the data camp was organised fully online. Nevertheless, there was still strong interest in the data camp as the school had received an overwhelming number of applications from all around the world, with different groups of participants, ranging from university students and working professionals. Eventually, 60 participants were selected from seven different countries (Singapore, Indonesia, Malaysia, Thailand, Vietnam, Taiwan, and China). Notably, a large percentage of the participants were accountants from the Big 4 accounting firms in Singapore, who were looking to upgrade themselves and learn new skills in digital technologies.

The curriculum design took into account the characteristics of online teaching that includes 12 hours of lectures and three hours of group project presentations; the content covered the latest trends in digitalisation and business model construction, introduction to Python programming, data analysis and visualisation, and the application in accounting and financial analytics.

The data camp exposed the participants to current trends in the accounting industry and equipped them with new skillsets through programming in Python. Hands-on exercises were conducted to train participants to be familiar with automating their jobs of retrieving and saving files through Python scripts. The ability to obtain publicly available information from Yahoo! Finance also proved useful for accountants as they may need to extract and visualise market trading data. Finally, descriptive statistics and regressions analysis were also taught as accountants need to infer from the data that they have obtained to make more informed decisions in their daily job.

Interactive and Engaging Online Group Presentation

Group project presentations, a hallmark of SMU teaching pedagogy, were a major feature of the online data camp. Participants were divided into project groups which required them to apply what they had learnt throughout the camp to perform analysis on a real company that they had selected and provide feasible suggestions on business model, digital transformation issues, and how accountants in that company could react in the "new normal" of a post-COVID-19 world. With face-to-face presentation rendered impossible, online interactive presentation had certainly made the data camp experience unique and more engaging.

Overall, the participants (both working professionals and students) had acquired hard technical skills and soft communication skills through novel online teaching as well as presentations; they had also expanded their network by getting to know new friends in the camp. Several participating in this course had described the online data camp as an *unforgettable experience*, something that they would recommend to fellow colleagues or friends.

The success of the first online data camp has encouraged SOA to continue to launch such a camp (the latest one being in February 2021) to provide regular training opportunities for accountants as well as to reinforce the importance of digital technology for existing accounting students. The dual-prong approach definitely supports the emphasis on upskilling and life-long learning.

Preparing a Future-Ready Accountant

According to a *Forbes* article "Why Artificial Intelligence is the Future of Accounting", many accounting tasks, which include tax, payroll, audits, and banking, will be fully digitalised using AI-based technology. Therefore, digital skills are required to complement technical accounting knowledge. Future-ready accountants will be doing more interpretation and communication of results to their clients, instead of doing only the mundane jobs of identifying, verifying, measuring, recording, and classifying transactions. These low-level operational jobs are likely to be outsourced or automated, and accountants are required to perform more value-adding tasks in analysis and interpretation.

In addition, accounting firms may be looking for data scientists who have the ability to understand and manipulate massive volumes of data; and combine operational, technical and financial data into rich data sets. Scenario planners will also be in high demand as these individuals have the ability to run several models simultaneously to determine the likelihood of certain scenarios happening.

Conclusions

To continue to thrive in the new roles in the digital age, universities will need to ensure that students possess both technical accounting knowledge and digital skills that prepare them for accounting jobs of the future. This means besides having a rigorous accounting-based education, universities should also teach skills that will allow students to navigate a future workplace where digital technologies are the norm. Employers must also continue to advocate and support their employees in upgrading their skills through regular training and education. This is especially important given that future developments in technology are likely to occur rapidly and require new skillsets to navigate.

Part 1 of this chapter was first published by CPA Australia in Charting the Future of Accountancy with AI under the chapter title "Grooming the next generation of accounting professionals for the age of artificial intelligence".

Part 2 of this chapter was first published as a Column by the UOB-SMU Asian Enterprise Institute under the title "Future-ready Accountant: Upskilling and Life-long Learning in the Age of Digital Transformation".

Printed in the United States
by Baker & Taylor Publisher Services

Printed in the United States
by Baker & Taylor Publisher Services